I0046689

New Insights into Prognostic Data Analytics in Corporate Communications

New Insights into Prognostic Data Analytics in Corporate Communications

Pragyan Rath
Indian Institute of Management Calcutta

K. Shalini
State Bank of India

BEP BUSINESS EXPERT PRESS

New Insights into Prognostic Data Analytics in Corporate Communications
Copyright © Business Expert Press, LLC, 2020.

All rights reserved. No part of this publication may be reproduced, stored in a retrieval system, or transmitted in any form or by any means—electronic, mechanical, photocopy, recording, or any other except for brief quotations, not to exceed 250 words, without the prior permission of the publisher.

First published in 2020 by
Business Expert Press, LLC
222 East 46th Street, New York, NY 10017
www.businessexpertpress.com

ISBN-13: 978-1-94744-110-1 (paperback)
ISBN-13: 978-1-94744-111-8 (e-book)

Business Expert Press Corporate Communication Collection

Collection ISSN: 2156-8162 (print)
Collection ISSN: 2156-8170 (electronic)

Cover and interior design by S4Carlisle Publishing Services Private Ltd., Chennai, India
Cover image by Billion Photos/shutterstock.com

First edition: 2020

10 9 8 7 6 5 4 3 2 1

Printed in the United States of America.

Abstract

The book advances diagnosis-prognosis models that mark antecedent frames in various commercial forms of communication—annual reports, investigative fiction–Poirot series, Sci-Fi, and advertisements. The authors thereby develop a study of "narrative markets" by proposing the "narrative of things" as the next innovative mega trend in business analytics. A unique feature of the book is the special section dedicated to industry-academic practitioners, who have offered a bird's-eye view in the Review Speak section of every chapter of this book: Prof. H. Gin Chong, Prairie View A&M University; Prof. Elena V. Orlova, Graduate School of Management, St. Petersburg University; Vishal Dhawan, CEO of Plan Ahead Wealth Advisors Pvt. Ltd; Dhrubojyoti Sinha, Associate Vice President, Kantar IMRB; Kim Lisson, Principal in Karrak Consulting; and Umesh Shrikhande, CEO, Taproot Dentsu. Industry-academic chapter contributors include Aman, Niteen, Shubhra, Vamshi, Pragyan, Anant, Karthi, Shalini, and Namit.

Keywords

narrative of things; narrative markets; annual reports; deconstruction; interpretive communities; sci-fi; Poirot; consumer questionnaire; ad agency; publicity; analytics

Contents

Acknowledgements

I thank the Indian Institute of Management Calcutta for providing financial support to my project "Pre-empting Market Trends through Narratives: Corporate Communications in a Competitive Market," which climaxed into the composition of this book.

Many thanks to Shalini, Aman, Niteen, Shubhra, Vamshi, Anant, Karthi, and Namit for the amazing contribution in the form of chapters.

My deepest gratitude to H. Chin Chong, professor of accounting and director of Executive MBA Program, Prairie View A&M University; Elena V. Orlova, head of Languages for Academic and Business Communication Department for Graduate School of Management, St. Petersburg University, Russian Federation; Vishal Dhawan, founder and CEO, Plan Ahead Wealth Advisors Pvt. Ltd; Dhrubojyoti Sinha, associate vice president, Kantar IMRB; Kim Lisson, principal, Karrak Consulting (www.karrak.com.au); and Umesh Shrikhande, CEO, Taproot Dentsu for their generous reviews on the contributions.

Thank you for helping us develop innovation in data analytics and communications.

Pragyan Rath

CHAPTER 1

Narrative Markets and Narrative Informatics

Pragyan Rath[1]

Review Speak

In this chapter, the author has skillfully developed analytical models for framing the narrative markets and the domain of narrative informatics. A narrative market consists of premeditated interpretive cues in strategic narratives, powerful executions by adept communication tools or media, projected reader responses, estimated cultural extrapolations, and formation of interpretive clusters. Each of these elements is explained and discussed in the chapter that eventually projects areas that need further research on cultural capital and genre production. This is a good reference for academicians, practitioners, and students.

—H. Gin Chong[2]

Differences in information processing, variety, and diversity of agents of communication who create, perceive, and consume narratives can easily lead to misinterpretation, poor diagnostics, and limited strategic thinking. The world as a huge narrative market awaits its analysis and interpretation and calls for groundbreaking ideas from different research and knowledge domain perspectives. The genre of narrative

---

[1]Pragyan Rath, Communications, Indian Institute of Management Calcutta.
[2]H. Gin Chong, professor of accounting and director of Executive MBA Program, Prairie View A&M University.

as a form of reconstructing reality into an imaginary world shared by interpretive communities will help companies develop their corporate strategies and introduce sustainable solutions; the way consumers interpret a narrative "drives their consumption and shapes their culture."

The narrator-producer needs new tools to create value "through the conversion of narratives into economic capital." The chapter draws on the traditional business megatrends: sustainability, disruptive technologies, market, and so on, and introduces new concepts of narrative markets, narrative informatics, and narrative of things as the foci of their research.

The author introduces a new method of analysis, a new analytical model that helps develop strategic market investigation. The model, called the Genre GPS, is the unique tool that opens new ways to explore the narrative markets. "The Genre GPS analysis is inevitable," argues the author, "to enable impactful corporate strategy by re-construing real and/or creative solutions via narrative-influences . . . to develop mega consumption trends across consumption clusters."

One of the strongest attractions of the research is the way the author lets her audience dive into the history of critical theory; the author introduces a compelling and illuminating review of theories and interpretations and creates fascinating links between different domains of knowledge and expertise. The names of Jacques Derrida, Stanley Fish, Marie-Laure Ryan, as well as John Berger, Herbert Marcuse, and Walter Benjamin in one research article on the narrative/genre for market value creation give a clear sense of the thought genesis and inspire not only the researchers but also a wider readership to follow the further development of narrative market studies.

—Elena V. Orlova[3]

The field of business communication has been pigeonholed into language skills. Yet language skills are an essential subset of the larger

---

[3]Elena V. Orlova, Head of Languages for Academic and Business Communication Department for Graduate School of Management St. Petersburg University, Russian Federation.

managerial function of problem diagnosis and solution development. In other words, communication is also about framing, positioning, and re-positioning, or perhaps "edging" problems for solutions. Edging likewise entails strategic formalities, and strategic formalism is again a subset of the larger issue of sustainable solutions. Sustainable solutions also necessitate systemic governance. And systemic governance in a dynamic market with an avalanche of disruptive technologies is the twenty-first century cat on a hot tin roof. So analysis of the tool of edging strategic problems for sustainable solutions, through the development of systemic governance in a market dominated by disruptive technologies is arguably the twenty-first century megatrend in business and management studies. This is even more evident in emerging markets and in markets that are reconciling the economic shift from labor-centric framings into consumer-centric positioning.

This book advances acquired models of diagnosis-prognosis that mark antecedent frames produced by various tools of strategic "edging"—annual reports, investigative fiction, science fiction/movies, and advertisements. These are identified as "narrative" domains to extract and develop understanding of how communications operationalize edging in "narrative markets." Douglas Holt has already popularized "myth markets."[4] Along the lines of the myth market composition, we constitute the narrative markets. The underlying assumption in both is how narratives shape and/or respond to the markets and in the process become tools of systemic governance. Considering the relevance of narratives in markets, we propose "narrative of things" as the mega-trend in business analytics equivalent to the more familiar "internet of things." In the process, we develop formalizing techniques in business analytics in the form of "narrative informatics" as an emerging subdomain of "art and cultural informatics." Informatics studies information as a channel for the production of narratives.[5] Information is channeled by and through narratives, and narratives are channeled by and through markets.

---

[4]D. Holt. 2004. *How Brands become Icons: The Principles of Cultural Branding* (Cambridge, MA: Harvard Business Review).

[5]"Art and Cultural Informatics." *Illinois Informatics.* December 31, 2018 https://www.informatics.illinois.edu/informatics-phd/art-and-cultural-informatics/

Research Gap: Interconvertibility between Narrative Structures and Market Structures

All narratives have formal properties. But narrative structures have corresponding market properties in terms of the value creation they project in their consumption practices. Neither marketing research nor narrative research has leveraged this interconvertibility of formal structures, resulting in the potentially disruptive diagnosis of mega-consumption patterns. Thus, corporate strategy may be reconstrued around the *narrative influences* that genres produce through various narrative tools corresponding to different consumption needs, thereby developing discernible consumption cultures. The identifiable clusters, on meticulous inspection, disclose macro consumption trends that may be leveraged in order to profile at analytical research levels distinctive cultural individualities as market equivalents of typical narrative designs. Using the interdisciplinary interconnectivity of markets and narratives, we attempt to develop schematics of strategic market investigation through a macroanalytical model, called the Genre GPS.

Through the method of the global positioning system, we can track travelers and develop geopolitical clusters. Through the Genre GPS, we can track the consumption need of developing, saturating, and disrupting of mega-consumption patterns in a market context. Consumption need can be identified or developed or transitioned from one type to another through the kind of narrative or the genre of storytelling that is being used for representation in the given system through particular narrative tools. Thus, the attempt in the chapter is to develop models of analytical strategies that make possible conversion of genres of representation into economic value creations by developing the concept of *interpretations* as the driving force of consumption culture:

> *How I interpret a narrative drives my consumption and shapes my culture.*

Interpretations are peculiar to the interpretive community whereby strategic narratives model reader responses prior to consumption. Powerful execution of the narrative through adept communication tools garner projected reader responses, thereby producing estimated cultural extrapolations conducive to sustenance or disruption of the market as planned by the market strategist. Figure 1.1 represents the nuanced formalities of the narrative market.

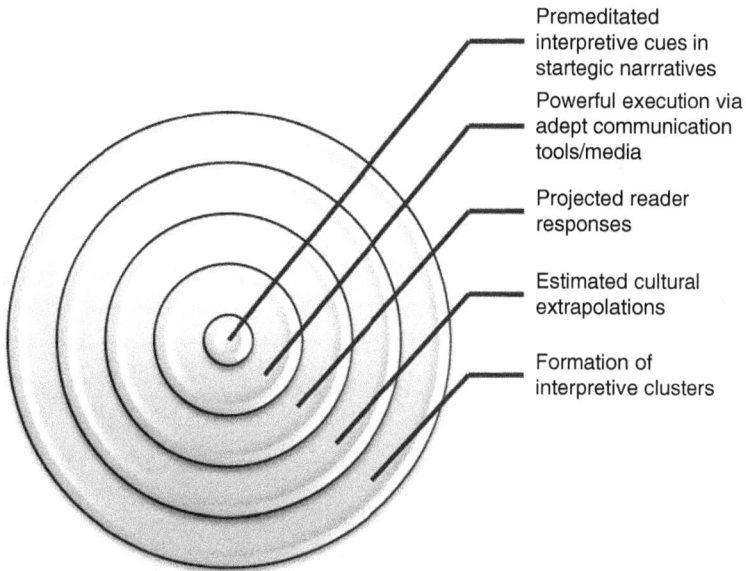

Figure 1.1 Constituents of narrative market

Thus, to enable impactful corporate strategy by reconstruing real and/ or creative solutions via *narrative influences* produced by *narrative types* and disseminated by narrative tools to develop mega-consumption trends across consumption clusters, the Genre GPS analysis is inevitable. In this maiden venture, we will concentrate on a few tools of narrative influencer disseminators in corporate spaces to develop nuanced models of narrative analytics, as briefly summarized in Figure 1.2.

Let us dive deep into the four nuanced analytical models of strategy of the edge in a narrative market.

Différance in the Narrative Market

Algerian-French poststructuralist Jacques Derrida's (1930–2004) contribution to the history of ideas is invaluable to business communication through his innovative nomenclature—**différance**. And this was possible

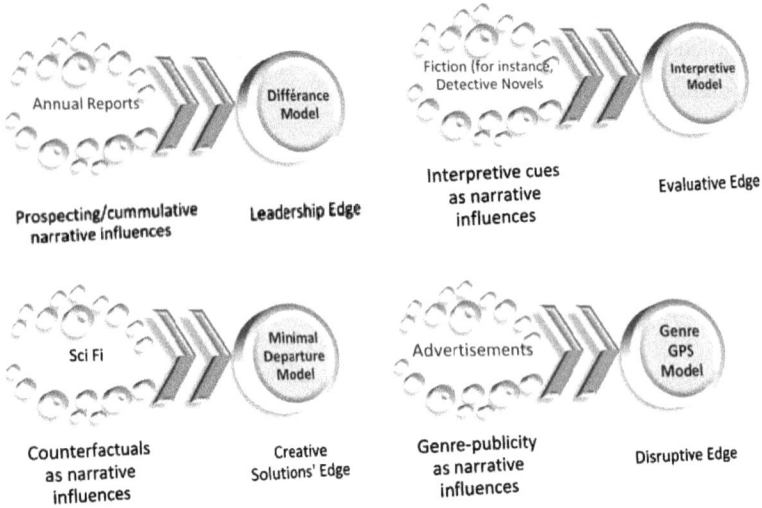

Figure 1.2 **Narrative tools and narrative influences**

through his pioneering interpretive method—deconstruction. He plays with two French words to develop the concept of **différance**.

- To defer: In the process of writing, in effect, meaning-making is always deferred. Until we write "t," "e," and "d," we do not know that the word is "ted." There are multiple possibilities after "t."

When we look at various organizational tools of communication, particularly annual reports, an interesting observation lies in their *futuristic* vision and mission statements—these are *deferred* actions. Such firms sport a *futuristic* leadership. In various forms of negotiations, deals, mergers, and conflicts, "promises" or "assurances" as the basis for negotiatory or conflicting outcomes are *deferred* realizations. Such narratives are *prospecting*. *Futuristic* and *prospecting* edges in communication platforms highlight a formal presence in a competitive market—a leadership presence that preempts a market future, that foresees emerging disruptions, and that prospects the future trends—in short, this is prognostic communications, heavy on strategy.

- To differ: A sign is a combination of signifier and signified. The signifier signifies or indicates the signified. The signified is the referent. It is the referencing signifier that welcomes a signified into existence. Without the signifier, the signified does not have an existence. For business communication, this is narrative in a competitive process of signification. Hence, the signifier develops into an important strategy for product/service positioning. It does not merely signpost the referent, thereby actualizing the referent in human memory by including the referent as a tangible item in the narrative market. The signifier also "edges" out other tangibles in a competitive market by differentiating the referent from other referents in a system of meaning-making.

We can find so many instances of the distinction factor in the self-positionings of firms in their annual reports. They predominantly create their distinctive value through their past activities, thus projecting a cumulative growth (the past adds on to the current value) through their unique, innovative, and distinctive competency projections.

Core competencies entail distinction. Distinction entails two aspects:

I differ from the rest, yet my distinction is legitimized not just by my difference from the rest but also by my unique "membership" into a unique community or group or association—the association with the best industry practices.

Such communications project the conformist and the conservative values of the firm in a fast, unreliable, change-afflicted market. For example:

I am "loyal" to my value; I have a definite path that I have been successfully traveling and still travel; I "conserve" my priorities, and hence I "prioritize" my core values over market disruptions.

In other words, the firm "markets" the aide-mémoire of its strong, dominant, and high credibility tradition in the market. This is the *inheritor* communicating; the heir to the throne of the best industry practice cluster.

Thus, the différance model of communication is a "play"[6] of significations, where the signifiers transition, transact, and transform between

---

[6]J. Derrida. 2009. "Structure, Sign, and Play in the Discourse of the Human Sciences." (*Writing and Difference*, trans. Alan Bass. London: Routledge, pp. 278–294). Hydra Design@ Peter Krapp. February 14, 2009. http://hydra.humanities.uci.edu/derrida/sign-play.html, (accessed June 1, 2018).

the *deferred* capital (that which will become economic value) and the *differed* capital (that which **is** economic value by virtue of its distinctions). A firm is *prospective* in its decision because of its prognostic strategist. A firm is cumulative in its propagations because of its inheritor-marketeer. And deconstruction is the diagnosis of this "play" between the *deferred* and the *differed* capital. Deconstruction is therefore reading the "play," deciphering the signals, symptoms, indications and consequences of the prognostic strategist and the inheritor-marketeer in their linguistic or visual depictions, illustrations, adaptations, proclamations, denials, and even absences and silences. For Derrida, the absences and silences are even more eloquent; they speak even more without speaking. Deconstruction is digging out the hidden potentialities that the linguistic or visual text contains, through its *deferring* and *differing* value propositions. Thereby, we propose the Play Strategy of Persuasive Communication that entails two kinds of players—the prognostic strategist and the inheritor-marketeer, as shown in Table 1.1.

Table 1.1 Play strategy of persuasive communication

Différance	Prognostic strategy	Différance	Inheritor-marketeer
To defer	Futuristic Prospecting Preempting Disruptions Strategy	To differ	Conserving Conforming Cumulating Core Competencies Marketing
	Deferred capital		Nostalgia

It is from the play strategy that the différance analytical model is developed, as is illustrated in Table 1.2.

Table 1.2 Différance analytical model

Mode of production/ consumption	Means of production	Appropriators of profit	Consumers	Strategy of profit
Decision/resolution • Prognostic strategist • Inheritor-marketeer	Différance • Prospecting communication • Cumulating communication	Producers of différance	Consumers of différance	Play

Interpretive Strategies in the Narrative Market

If Derrida discusses "play," then Stanley Fish,[7] the American literary theorist, discusses the playground—the interpretive communities. We will interpret a narrative according to the interpretive community to which we belong. The strategist here "edges" cues or anchors that shape interpretation. These strategic cues and anchors call into being the interpretive mechanism that will eventually deploy the reader to "interpret" the text through the parameters predetermined by the strategist. In other words, the strategist has already encoded the interpretive scheme against which the reader will now evaluate the meaning of the text in search of the narrative truth. In this capacity, the reader-writer forms an association—they form the interpretive community, and the distinction of being in that community is developed by the interpretive correspondence. Interpretive strategy then is the psycho-symbolic anchors in the narrative through which the reader is called into evaluating chronicles to produce "predetermined" interpretations. The obvious output is the interpretation, but the strategy is to develop narratives that will lead to **implied** interpretation.

Let us consider the 2010 Indian advertisement—"Pleasure—Hero Honda, Why should boys have all the fun?" The context is the patriarchal setting in India. When a boy goes out of the house, the mother does not ask about his whereabouts. When the sister goes out, each member of the family has a query. *Where are you going? When will you be back? What is the plan today?* So *Pleasure* speaks to all Indian girls: *despite the questions, have fun (pun intended). After all, why should boys have all the fun?* A strategist with a patriarchal agenda would demand into being the *interpretive correspondences* that would compel the reader (the emerging market consumer) to construe the narrative of *"why should boys have all the fun"* as a verdict on women empowerment. Feministic ideology may be the tactical criterion against which the verdict is evaluated—*women are equal to men.* Yet the interpretive scheme strategically positions "man" as the benchmark of the evaluation—*if men have fun, so should women, and with similar consumable products or services—bikes in this case specifically designed*

[7]S. Fish. "'Interpretive Communities.' From "'Interpreting the Variorum.'" In *The Norton Anthology of Theory & Criticism.* 2nd ed., eds. V. B. Leitch and W. W. Cain. New York, NY: Norton, 1974–1992 (1988–1992). pp. 1990–1991.

for empowered girls—but empowered because they get to do what boys do. So the benchmark matrix actually furthers the cause of the patriarchal community, but the identity is now repositioned as a woman-concerned community.

In short, the analyst looks for predetermined interpretations through strategic narrative edges. As analysts, we must hunt for benchmarks, evaluations, and parameters in similar narratives, a very plausible strategy used in detective fiction. The detective understands the interpretive cues of the suspects, and hence the interrogation is strategized around the interpretive concept. Table 1.3 depicts the interpretive strategy model.

Table 1.3 Interpretive strategy model

Mode of production/ consumption	Means of production	Appropriators of profit	Consumers	Governance logic of strategy of profit
Interpretive communities	Interpretive strategies	Producers of interpretive strategies	Consumers of interpretive strategies	Interpretive scheme (evaluation/ benchmark matrix)

Minimal Departure Model in Narrative Markets

Independent scholar Marie-Laure Ryan works in narratology and cyber culture, with the aim of furthering the principles of interpretive communities. Her article "Fiction, Non-Factuals, and the Principle of Minimal Departure" (1980) is a game changer in contemporary discussions on business communication. Fiction and its many forms through various media—movies, physical books, Kindle, sitcoms, and other versions of narratives—have not only been topics for central debates for *interpretive communities* but also one of the major trigger points for their formation. Hence, this club of interpreters of any form of fiction has been immersed in the *ways of narrating the fiction* as well. Ryan says that fiction is an alternate or possible world, alternate to the actual world we live in. And readers in the actual world, when they interpret the alternate world, do so by familiarizing the unfamiliar world—they connect the alternate and impossible factors in the fiction with the world they are living in. The connection is all about finding similarities, known referents, and the extent of the search for familiarity is through the reconstruction of the alternate world "as being the closest possible to the reality we know."[8]

Let us understand the traditional view of fiction—it is a made-up nonfactual event, an event that has never happened. Yet even fiction has actual world statements such as "On the twenty-ninth of May [1812] Napoleon left Dresden," a sentence that appears in Tolstoy's historical novel *War and Peace*."[9] Hence, Ryan concludes,

> This means that we will project upon the world of the statement everything we know about the real world, and that we will make only those adjustments which we cannot avoid. For instance, if somebody says: "If horses had wings they would be able to fly," we reconstrue an animal presenting all the properties of real horses, but which, in addition, has wings and is able to fly. We perform the same operation when we read in a fairy tale about a flying horse, when a child tells us "Last night I dreamed about a flying horse," and when a poet writes a sonnet about riding the flying horse of imagination.[10]

This action of readers "projecting all that we know, except for the few adjustments we cannot avoid" is equivalent to Ryan's conceptualization of the *principle of minimal departure*. Fiction criticism has always been centered on the newness of the style of telling a story—the novel way of narrating. But Ryan concentrates on the basic human culture of interpretation—we interpret through the projection of all that we know onto all that is not known. Thus, critical appreciation of the "new" may come from the "maximal" departure from the norm, but interpretation is concurrently through all that we know—the "minimal" departure from the known. Hence, when we read or enjoy fiction, what we "unconsciously" also imbibe is the way the narrative flows—the plot structure. This structure is important because fiction/narratives are nonfactual or counterfactual ways of solving problems. So stories, fiction, narratives,

---

[8]Ibid., 403.
[9]Ibid., 404.
[10]Ibid., 406.

counterfactuals, nonfactuals are alternate ways of understanding conflicts. For instance, George Orwell's famous *Animal Farm* is well known for its real-time references to actual world politics. Fables, allegories, suspense, science fiction, thrillers, romances, satires, realism, and many more are different modes, forms, and genres of stories. But the interpretive capacity of the individual is about the principle of "minimal departure," even if the intellectual aptitude is about "maximal departure."[11]

Now, an interpretive community is all about a community interpreting a nonfactual. Hence, the minimal departure interpretive process is inherent even in the interpretive methods, as is the maximal departure in the intellectual process, used for innovative placement of the community in a market high on intellectual sign-value.

So, let us say, intellectual value is a sign-value produced by a maximal departure interpretive process (cultural process), while human understanding is a minimal departure interpretive process. Either way, nonfactuals are creative processes of developing solutions. Ryan says elsewhere, "The pragmatic purpose of counterfactuals is not to create alternate possible worlds for their own sake, but to make a point about the actual world."[12] This shows that counterfactuals also "add" to what reality is perhaps missing, while the reader uses reality to navigate through the unreal world of the alternate world of fiction. Ryan talks about linguistic terms like "non-factive predicates"[13]: "I believe," "he thinks," "she wishes" as opposed to "I realize," "he knows," "she is aware of."

Stretching Ryan's linguistic horizon to grammatical moods, subjunctives are also interesting counterfactuals that add to real conditions:

> I may wish often that this was a world that had no poverty. Of course, this is fiction, yet the reality is a world with poverty. So as an interpreter I understand the fiction world minus poverty through the projection of my realistic knowledge of the actual poverty-ridden world. Yet, the wishful thinking is my creative solution to a concrete real time problem—a poverty-less world.

---

[11]Maximal departure is our coinage as against Ryan's "minimal departure".

[12]M. L. Ryan. 1991. *Possible Worlds, Artificial Intelligence, and Narrative Theory.* Bloomington, IN: Indiana UP, p. 48.

[13]Ryan, 1980, 406.

Similarly, in business communication, if I have to refuse a refund request, I resort to using a non-factive predicate or a subjunctive[14]:

Had the contract been more accurately set within the new budget rules, the incentive would have doubled itself." Realistically speaking, all I am saying is that I am not paying you the incentive!

As Ryan would say,

A sentence such as "John believes that horses have wings and are able to fly" normally means to the hearer that the object of John's belief resembles real world horses on all counts, except for the properties of having wings and being able to fly.[15]

So the minimal departure principle opens up an understanding of the equation between the projection of the factuals and the adjustment with the counterfactuals, and the degree of relatability between the two decides the kind of *narrative-influence* construed. The *narrative-influence* in a narrative market develops into the genre of the narrative.

Similarly, the interpretive community built around *narrative-influence* (we like science fiction, or we like thrillers) becomes a culture immersed in this relatability between the factuals and the nonfactuals:

the relationship between the two worlds is constitutive of genre: to know that a text is a fairy tale or a legend, a science fiction story or a historical romance, is to know, at least approximately, which aspects of the real world will be shared by the fictional world.[16]

Thus, the *genre of the narrative* is important information in a narrative market because it projects the kind of *narrative-influence* that shapes the cognition (interpretive skills) of the community consuming the genre.

---

[14]For more on subjunctive mood as pataphysical (artistic) solution to corporate communication problems like refusal to incentives at the cost of client appraisal, refer to P. Rath and A. Bharadwaj. 2018. "You've got Mail: Strategy in Style." In *Communication Strategies for Corporate Leaders: Implications for the Global Market*. London, UK: Routledge, pp. 109–119.

[15]Ryan, 1980, 406.

[16]Ibid., 415.

Research Hypothesis

So a consumer cluster is actively trained to be open to a certain degree of creative solutions because of its immersion in the type of counterfactual culture. If we know the desired degree of the creative solution, we would know the counterfactual culture that the interpretive community is immersed in; we would know how to replicate the imaginary solution as a real solution in the real world. *Narrative-Influence* then is about mapping the degree of relatability between the projection and the adjustment, between the factual and the nonfactual, between the real and the imaginary. Based on this relatability, we develop four levels of genres of narratives or plot structures that interpretive communities are immersed in and hence establish how to replicate imaginary solutions for real problems for that community.

Level 1: Nonsense Plot Structure

When there is a total lack of relatability between the factual and the counterfactual, the narrative constitutes itself into nonsense lyrics. Ryan states Lewis Carroll's nonsense poem in *Through the Looking-Glass*. We can imagine the interpretive community that grows around nonsense lyrics. The narratives in nonsense plots, through the obliteration of minimal departure and maximization of maximal departure, offer similar kinds of solutions in communities whose interpretive skills are construed around these kinds of fiction. The creative impact is the highest here. This would be the most hyperreal culture, with an extreme probability of high disruptive strategy—the Ryan hyperreal is the maximal departure at an all-time high:

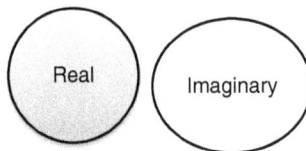

Level 2: Fairy Tale/Science Fiction Plot Structure

When there is an overlap between the two worlds, such that propositions are common to both the worlds, we get the next genre of plot structures. There are propositions only true for the fictional world, as in the X area marked as X in the diagram that follows, and with the following properties:

A) Untrue in factuals

B) Indeterminate in the counterfactual

Then there are those only true for the real world, as in Y area of the following figure, and with the following properties:

A) False in counterfactual

B) Indeterminate in factuals

The overlap, marked XY, reflects propositions that are true to both the real and the imaginary worlds.

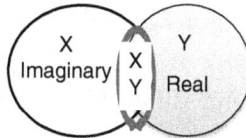

This is the fairy tale genre, which Ryan describes as close to the preindustrial concept of the world; or the science fiction/superhero fiction that describes a scientific concept of the world. Now imagine the solutions provided in fairy tales, and through the principle of minimal departure, attempt similar solutions in the interpretive communities where interpretive skills are construed around these kinds of fiction. The creative solutions' impact is significant, and the strategy is more disruptive. The *narrative-influence* is more of a subjunctive mood—this is the creative strategy of a wishful escape from the real into a "nostalgia" of an unreal reality. This is a cluster high on brand culture.

Level 3: Realistic/Historical Plot and Minimal Departure

Here, the factual is contained in the counterfactual, as in realistic fiction having factual historical and geographical content:

> In a realistic novel, the only difference between the real and the fictional world is that the latter includes additional members, namely the imaginary characters of the novel.[17]

Thus, everything true of the real world is equally true of the fictional world. But everything true of the fictional world is not necessarily true

---

[17]Ibid.

of the real world. The untrue propositions are "added" elements in the fictional world, with referents in the fictional world, as illustrated in the following diagram.

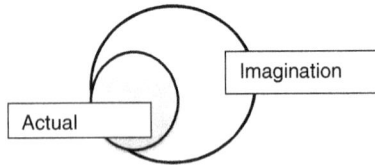

In this system, the creative solutions' impact is minimal, the strategy is moderately creative, and the *narrative-influence* is more prone to marketing cultures. The strategy is that of a high level of minimal departure.

Level 4: Impersonations and Minimal Departure

The final genre is the near total overlap of the fiction and the real. Ryan offers the example of the Socrates dialogues by Plato:

> Socrates is an impersonated speaker with respect to Plato, but he is a member of the same world, and everything he says is to be taken as true, or as potentially true, in the actual world.[18]

Here, unlike the fairy tale, the unreal propositions have to be integrated by the audience into the world she or he is reconstruing. In the impersonations, false propositions may be interpreted as inferior judgment and may be discarded from the reader's interpretation of the actual world. In the diagram that follows, the white circle depicts imagination, and the grey circle represents the actual world.

---

[18]Ibid., 418.

So, using Ryan's minimal departure principle, we have devised a strategy of the counterfactual in persuasion, as is illustrated in Table 1.4.

It is from the strategy of the counterfactual that the minimal departure model can be developed, as is illustrated in Table 1.5.

Table 1.4 Strategy of the counterfactual in persuasion

Interpretive culture	Genre (narrative-influence)	Interpretive process	Solution	Strategy
Hyperreal (ahistorical)	Nonsense plot	Maximal departure (intellectual, abstract)	High creative solutions	Strategy of the hyperreal
Brand culture (high on nostalgia)	Fairy tale	Significant minimal departure	Significant creative solutions	Strategy of the neoreal
Marketing culture (moderately real)	Historical, legendary, realistic	Minimal departure	Minimal creative solutions	Strategy of the neoreal (more towards real)
Realistic culture (rooted in reality)	Impersonations	High minimal departure	Prescriptive solutions	Strategy of the real

Table 1.5 Minimal departure analytical model

Mode of production/ consumption	Means of production	Appropriators of profit	Consumers	Strategy of profit
Interpretive culture • Hyperreal • Brand culture • Marketing culture • Realism	Genres • Nonsense • Fairy tale • Historical, legend, realistic • Impersonations	Producers of genres	Consumers of genres	Counterfactual strategy (the relation between minimal departure and maximal departure)

The Genre GPS Strategy Model

John Berger in his iconic British Broadcasting Corporation (BBC) episodes and in the eventual best seller *Ways of Seeing* (1972)[19] devised a genre

---

[19]J. Berger and M. Dibb. 1972. *Ways of Seeing* (London: BBC Enterprises).

template for narratives. In the history of narrative theory, Berger hardly makes the cut because the criteria for genre division have more to do with formal properties of narrative structure. But with Berger, there is a marked departure. His division parameter highlights a very crucial point of departure—the economic valorization that the genre intends to exchange its artistic form with, and the intent here is not the story or the methods of the story being told—the intent is more to do with the economic value the story and its forms intend to fulfill. To understand the economic value of narratives, we have to go through the history of critical/literary theory to understand the genesis of genre valorization. Critical theory posits two strong thinkers who play a significant role in helping us reposition Berger's genre template as an economic template of concern.

Critical Theory: A History of Sorts

Critical theory has come a long way in helping to understand art and its types as market evaluations. It started with Marx in a big way, and the Frankfurt School of Critical Thinking institutionalized the criterion of art as an economic tool of consumption and governance. Two Frankfurt thinkers, Herbert Marcuse and Walter Benjamin, are significantly important in this article's scheme of things.

Marcuse and the Affirmative Character of Culture

Herbert Marcuse in his *Negations* (1968)[20] discusses the "affirmative character of culture" function. He states that a culture takes a utilitarian view of art. Art is understood as a parallel universe, a possible world, an alternate reality, wherein lie higher values of the human world, the conditional options, the wishful thinking, and the grand narratives—the untouched parameters of human conduct of goodness, virtue, and beauty. Art functions as that wishful world where we as human beings may enjoy our greater order of existence—the existence of goodness. But once out of that world, back into the economic transactions of daily lives, we continue with our transactional and mundane nature of existence. The contradiction is what is interesting to us. The very same economic forces

---

[20]H. Marcuse. 1968. *Negations: Essays in Critical Theory* (London, UK: Free Association Books).

produce the composition of virtues in that possible world—the world of art where everything is beautiful, good and true, and a far cry from the world of economics, where everything is banal, brutal, and utilitarian. Hence, to maintain the human faith in the better form of human consciousness, art functions as the unifying technology that helps affirm the culture to an artistic consensus of human virtues. Diagrammatically, Figure 1.3 explains the affirmative character of culture.

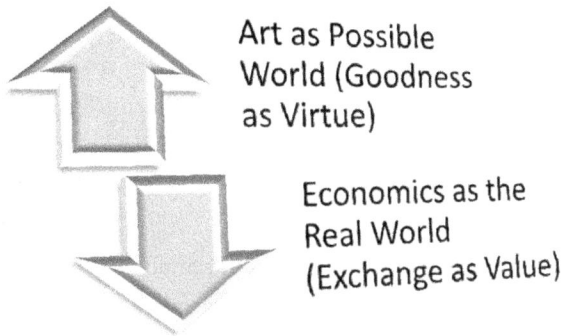

Art as Possible World (Goodness as Virtue)

Economics as the Real World (Exchange as Value)

Figure 1.3 Affirmative character of culture

Benjamin and the Aura versus Envy Phenomenon

Walter Benjamin in "The Work of Art in the Age of Mechanical Reproduction"[21] discusses the social production of sentiment through the work of art—predominantly, he identifies two kinds. He says that aura is a social condition of collective feeling that emerges when the object of aura has a halo around it—the object is beyond reach because it is enigmatic and distanced, and its means of production are invisible. In other words, the aura is apparently there for intrinsic qualities within the object—qualities that only the object of aura can have, and thereby the object is bestowed with a unique, authentic, and distinctive quality of existence that can only be admired but not possessed by the onlookers.

On the other hand, there is envy. Envy is a social collective feeling that emerges for an object of some altitude but more so because of the wish to displace it. The reason for its exalted altitude is not its intrinsic virtue but the technology it has used to create value for itself. In other words, the

---

[21]W. Benjamin and J. Underwood. 2008. *The Work of Art in the Age of Mechanical Reproduction* (London, UK: Penguin).

means of production of its animated social position is apparently evident. Thus the onlooker can aspire for the same, with the conditional criterion of success being the tool or the possession of the material value that gave the object this grand social position. Now, what happens to the object of envy? It evaluates its position in terms of the social envy that is produced for it by the paradoxically aspirational class—the very class of people who think they can displace the object of envy by acquiring the material benefits, the acquisition of which got the object to its esteemed position. On the other hand, the object basks in the envy creation because it feels validated in its successful social position through the acquisition of materiality that gives it this position, yet the materiality is merely the technology; it is more the production of envy that creates value for the position—the position is not aspirational if it is not enviable! Hence, to be aspirational, the position has to appear achievable. And yet to be enviable, the position has to delude the acquiring of it, and the affirmation of not acquiring it has to come from the narrative: that the lack of acquiring the material technology is the only reason for the inequality. Figure 1.4 depicts the complex inverse propor-tion of the aura and envy social production of value creation.

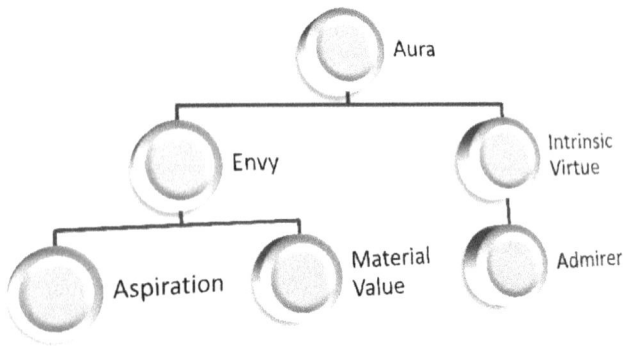

Figure 1.4 Aura and envy social production of value creation

From Critical Theory to Sociology to Economics

It was Pierre Bourdieu who revolutionized the Marx notion of economic capital into cultural capital in his oft quoted "Forms of Capital" (1986).[22]

---

[22]P. Bourdieu. 1986. *The Forms of Capital by Pierre Bourdieu.* [Online] Marxists.org. https://www.marxists.org/reference/subject/philosophy/works/fr/bourdieu-forms-capital.htm, (accessed April 4, 2015).

Culturally, sociologically, and otherwise, it all started with the feudal system and art. High art was the possession of the acquirers of the economic capital. Thus, people with art were people with cultural capital: artistic value was directly proportional to economic value. The rich had art embodied in their life, their way of living, and this embodiment was translated as legacy through generations. This is the least transactional form of culture; it is the most preserved form. This is embodied capital. With the bourgeoisie capturing the market and thereby leading to the collapse of the aristocrats, cultural capital started becoming transactional in terms of obtaining objects of value—this developed into objectified capital. With time new institutions developed, and these institutions defined values—this came to be institutionalized capital. With the era of technology entering and disturbing class systems, what we get is the prominence of cultural capital—what was originally an add-on to economic wealth or a by-product of it is now a substitute for it. So social status is determined by cultural capital and not necessarily economic capital, and so is the shift from economic positioning to a cultural positioning. Figure 1.5 represents the transition of economic capital into cultural capital.

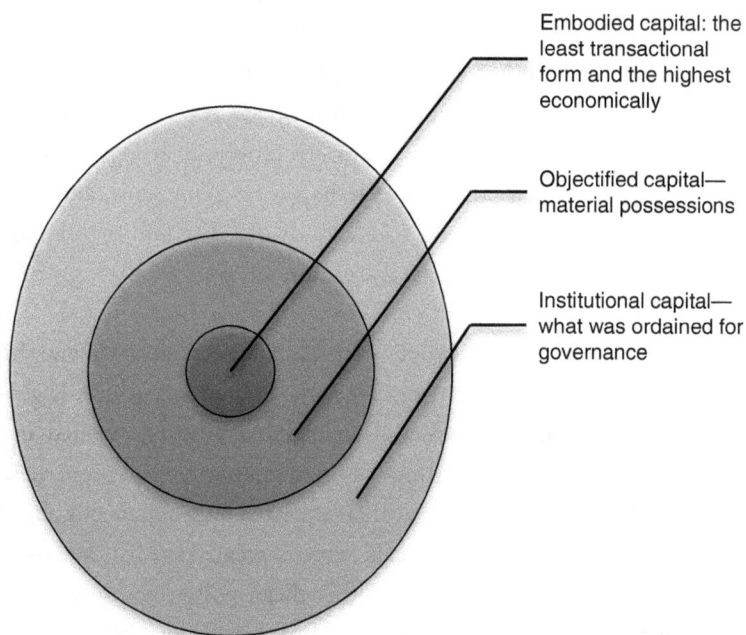

Embodied capital: the least transactional form and the highest economically

Objectified capital—material possessions

Institutional capital—what was ordained for governance

Figure 1.5 Transition of economic into cultural capital forms

Berger and Narrative Genres

Berger extracted the prominent forms of narrative representations through the most famous medium of representation then—the oil paintings. These are studied from the representation forms of the foundational era of consumerism, more popularly known as the Age of Reason. He found the parallel of these genres in the more modern form of consumerism with the more modern tool of representation—cheap color photography in commercials. The highest form of genre was the history painting. The rich patrons chose artists to represent them through legacy or mythological or historical episode, but the intention was not to represent these legacies, but to translate the legacy as a representative of the patron himself or herself. In other words, the mythological figure represented the patron in the "ideal" world of art. Thus, the genre depicted the ideal pose. The "icon" was an idealized representation of the spectator-buyer.

Then emerged the portraiture, where the personality was surrounded with and by his or her objectified capital—the bureaucratic pose. Thus, the material around the person increased social status. The person was individualized depicting the rise in economic category, but at the same time distanced, typically portrayed as looking through you.

Then, the genre representations arrived. These were cheaper forms of idealized community/collective representations of the mass—the common people—who have not climbed up the economic ladder, but the hope in human goodness is very much alive and strong. These depicted the sentimental pose—"we are happy, working hard, and praying that the higher power will take care of us." The sentimental pose advocated survival rather than disruption of systems through rebel forms of upheaval.

Then, emerged the landscapes with the property pose—ownership and the mileage one can get from what the community thinks is good ownership. Even the livestock and architecture were represented in a manner that showcased ownership—as if animals were mere properties.

Then, there were the still lives. These depicted only objects but objects presented as subjects of art. Thus, the concupiscence pose, or the pose of sin, but a lesser sin was developed. This cheap possession of objects as art subjects was an addition to the world of conspicuous consumption. Figure 1.6 illustrates the hierarchy of genres.

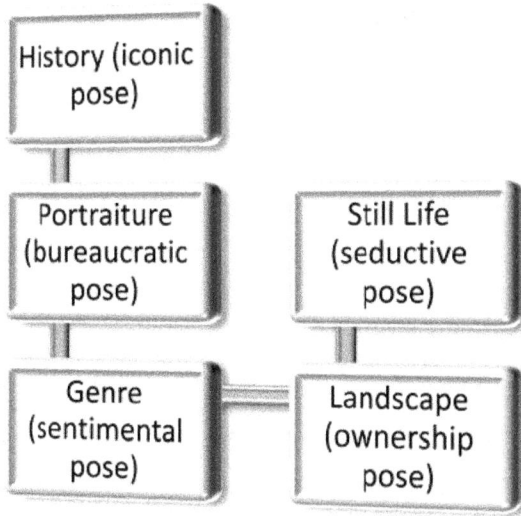

Figure 1.6 Hierarchy of genres

Language of Publicity: Berger

It was Berger who theorized on the social construct of the greatest tool of modern mode of representation, the language of consumerism—publicity. Publicity is the language of economic capital, albeit deferred. Unlike oil paintings, advertisements showed not what is there today, but what the spectator-buyer can achieve if she or he buys the object that would help the person enter the deferred lifestyle. Thus, publicity is nothing but deferred economic capital. And this condition of deferred economic capital is nothing but manufacture of mass social envy. And this condition of being looked at enviously by the masses is called glamour. Publicity converts personal envy into mass envy through the manufacture of glamour, as illustrated in Figure 1.7.

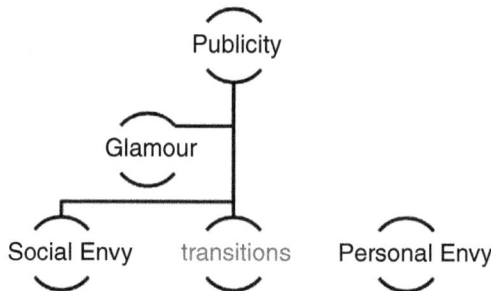

Figure 1.7 Grammar of publicity

Research Proposition: Scope of a Nuanced Form of Representational Strategy

Berger mentioned how a personal emotion transitions into a collective mass emotion, and the manufacture of that emotion at a mass level thus becomes the means of crowd control. Now let us translate crowd control into Marcuse's affirmative character of culture, mass emotion into the Benjamin aura-envy phenomenon, and mass emotion into economic emotion by cultural capital, and the entire set of transitions modeled by the narrative genre type. Thus, we get a nuanced form of representational strategy, where the type of representation creates a mass emotion, which is economically viable. So in history paintings, the idealized pose creates a social function called aura-glamour and thereby a substitute of economic capital—embodied capital. This is affordable by the rich spectator-buyer. Table 1.6 shows the correspondence map of all the connections. We call this the affirmative consumption segmentation.

In a consumer society, social function of art is glamour, and thus, if we can map the glamour with the narrative genre, then we can measure the potential capital developed for a consumer market. Table 1.7 illustrates the value of glamour. And this value creation also depicts the hierarchy of the economic aspirational sectors.

Findings: The Industrial Market versus the Corporate Market Contrast

Let us map the affirmative strategy and the value creation of publicity with contemporary commercials in different industry/market domains, as represented in Table 1.8.

Generally niche and luxury products have the aura built around them through their legacy/historical/mythological projection. The British royalty still uses its embodied capital to project its superior existence to a mass spectator. Jewelry commercials use "envy" to establish the spectator-buyer's deferred social position. An interesting episode is the contrast between the famous Lux and Dove soap representations in Indian advertising. Lux brand uses big celebrities to position the use of the soap with envy. If the spectator-buyer uses Lux, she or he will have the

Table 1.6 *The consumption segmentation*

Genre	Spectator-buyer	Affirmative character of culture			Personal emotion into mass emotion = glamour
		Possible world	Referent	Symbolic pose	
History	Social capital (rich)	Icon history/legacy	You	Idealized view to support own view: **idealized pose**	Aura
Portraiture	Social capital (upper middle class, rich, gradually middle class)	Your consolidated status with all things you own visually there with your presence	You	**Bureaucratic pose**	Envy
Genre	Mass market	If not the market, a higher power will take care of you	You (through the idealized pose of your community)	**Sentimental pose**	Sentimentalism
Landscape	Mass market	Celebration of private property	You (more focus on what you own, particularly land and architecture)	**Utility pose** Conspicuous consumption	Mileage
Still life	Mass market	Common object converted into Object d'Art (object of art)	You (through your artistic taste)	**Seductive pose**	Concupiscence (lesser sin that may be forgiven)

Table 1.7 *Value of glamour*

Genre	Function of art = glamour	What is the status of the means of production and the fate of the aspiration of the economic segment?	Corresponding capital formation
History	Aura	Not visible, neither the tool nor the outcome easily exchangeable	Embodied capital
Portraiture	Envy	Visible, the tool is mass reproduced but not the outcome, not necessarily, but economic segment may or may not change	Objectified capital
Genre	Sentimentalism (esteem)	Not visible, tool is grand narratives, the outcome is not mass reproducible (you stay in the same economic segment)	Institutionalized capital
Landscape	Mileage (esteem)	Visible, limited reproducibility (economic segment may change)	Institutionalized capital
Still life	Seduction (esteem)	Visible, mass reproducible, but you stay in the same economic segment	Objectified capital

Table 1.8 *Publicity through affirmative consumption*

	Glamour	Genre	Industries
Publicity	Aura	History	Niche products/royalty
	Envy	Portraiture	Jewelry, Lux
	Sentimentalism	Genre	Bajaj/Insurance/Chetan Bhagat books, Dove soap as pitched against Lux soap
	Mileage (esteem)	Landscape	Tourism, acquisitions
	Seduction (esteem)	Still life	E-commerce

life that the celebrity has. But in the contemporary multinational corporate era, the impact of the celebrity as aspirational may not work on many audience segments. Dove for instance positions the normal women through its genre narrative of sentimentalism—"we are beautiful as we are." Chetan Bhagat brought about a revolution by writing like and for the common people—again genre sentimentality.

Tourism is more into depicting the kind of landscapes the destination owned. Dan Brown projects landscapes and genres in his best sellers.

Post-acquisition narratives in the e-commerce world depict landscape of products and services, for consumers now to re-own. These e-commerce sites are replete with their countless glorious seductively posed objects.

Disruptive Glamour

But what about populations that are no longer enamored by celebrities, or who do not buy into sentimental lies. The disruptive glamour introduced into the market corresponds to self-actualization needs—the need to search for one's true identity—the need to be different from even celebrities (both aura and envy), and also from your community (genre). Self-actualization as a need emerges when the economic growth starts disrupting the set hierarchy. As mentioned, embodied capital loses its sheen, envy is now mass reproducible, and hence everyone has access to the material-tool that would eventually propel the spectator-buyer into a better economic position.

So, what happened to people in the upper crust of the economic strata who have their aesthetic pose and hence their intrinsic cultural capital now appropriated by the lower economic segments? By this mass appropriation and hence class neutralization, these consumers are left to fend for themselves in a world of clones, robots, mass neutralization and standardization, and homogenization. Their differential sense of being unique and exclusive is lost upon the market—hence, here we have a personal emotion that has the potential for mass reproduction—a new breed of emotion—that can disrupt the hierarchy of aura and envy—and this is self-actualization. Thus, brands come in with symbolic poses that have abstract representations, and these abstract representations "only" lend themselves to these "segregated" and "ghettoed" people, whom time and technology and economics have been passing over. So here is the new disruptive technology in affirmative consumerism as illustrated by Table 1.9.

Birth of the New Genre: How to Disrupt the Consumer Market through Symbolic Narrative

The clown character in the *Batman* series is the greatest of abstract symbols—it refers to itself. So abstract advertising uses abstract language

Table 1.9 *Disruptive conversion of aura/envy into self-actualization = disruptive affirmative strategy*

Genre	Old glamour	Social gap for leveraging disruption	New disruptive glamour (new social condition)	New symbolic pose	Corresponding capital formation
History	No more aura for embodied capital	People are climbing economic segments at least through cultural capital	Self-actualize (empowerment)	**Gesamtkunstwerk** Absolute experience, aesthetic experience, relation to the brand, to each other, to their life-world, and to themselves	All forms of capital Institutionalized capital
Portraiture	Envy is useless Now tools of distinction are mass reproduced	Dilution of cultural hierarchy which earlier caused envy			

to make sense to the consumer segment looking for distinction from mass reproduction. And hence this new form of language that is not mass reproducible elevates the distinctive ability of interpretation. Hence, envy and aura are converted into a self-actualized symbolic value—where the need is to "experience" oneself in the complete act of making meaning, an "experience" that only art can bring about. The German word is *Gesamtkunstwerk*—the complete aesthetic experience. And yet the winning hand in value creation is the institutionalizer of the *Gesamtkunstwerk.*

Research Proposition: Gesamtkunstwerk Value Creation for Sustenance in an Oversaturated Market

When mass saturation is reached, value differentiation is a requirement, and the value differentiator will reap profits through identification of the affirmative needs of the consumer segment. Once the needs are identified, the existing need is transitioned into the disruptive affirmation positioning through corresponding narrative styles. Thus, in a system, the value creator is the need differentiator, the means of value creation is transition of glamour, and the consumers are the spectator-buyers whose needs the transitional glamour converts into aspirations. Thus, a system of economic neutralization produces genres of narratives with corresponding economic values. Thus, every system has an underlying economic logic of disruption/sustenance, and that is what we call the affirmative logic of the publicity template. Figure 1.8 illustrates the genre-publicity template for value creation, or what we can nickname as the Genre GPS.

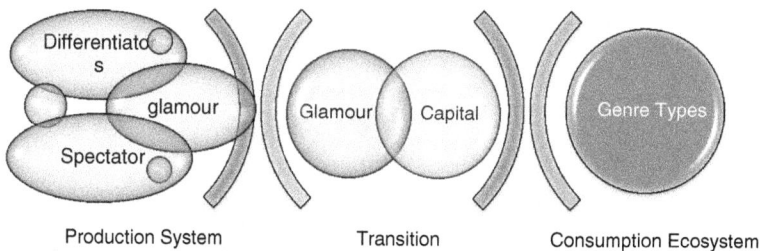

Figure 1.8 Genre GPS

Future Research Possibilities

The Genre GPS explains the unlimited possibilities of consumer study and marketing, and branding and value creation. What kind of narrative would unfold what kind of mass emotion and hence what kind of mass emotion produces what kind of social phenomenon in terms of the kind of glamour created and, with the kind of glamour created, the kind of capital formulation developed—this identification of the reigning form of cultural capital will project three circumstances to the differentiator:

A) How the current cultural capital reigns supreme.
B) Whether the current cultural capital is on the verge of disruption in terms of the saturation of social emotion.
C) When to bring in the disruptive technology of genre production, once saturation is identified.

Thus, the Genre GPS will help pitch the narrator-producer as the market surplus value creator through the conversion of narratives into economic capital. To add to the Genre GPS method, one has to develop the methodology of narrative scanning and analysis, and that is the future project for narrative market analysis.

CHAPTER 2

A Deconstruction of Annual Reports

Aman Narang,[1] Niteen Bali,[2] and Shubhra Chaudhry[3]

Review Speak

Annual reports have over the years been favored as the best place to go to for serious investors trying to make investment or divestment decisions with respect to a particular company. The focus of these reports has largely been on the quantitative aspects, which are backward looking and mostly reflect on the past, making them of limited use for a large number of readers. A more recent shift has been to use annual reports for qualitative as well as quantitative messaging. This approach provides a peek into the future as viewed through the lens of the company, reveals the strategic view of the business, and portrays the company as differentiated enough to appeal to different stakeholders. This chapter includes case studies of some well-known Indian companies and the evolution of their annual reports over successive years. This case study approach reveals how these companies have influenced their stakeholders and used differentiated communication strategies and themes to stand out from their peer group and competitors. The framework that has been created on multiple metrics will be very helpful in creating

[1]Aman Narang, Manager, Yes Accelerator, Yes Bank.
[2]Niteen Bali, Manager, Business Technology Transformation, Reliance Commercial Finance.
[3]Shubhra Chaudhry, Associate Manager, Vedanta, Sesa Goa Iron Ore.

corporate communication that achieves the desired positioning among stakeholders. I am confident that by using this framework, annual reports that can otherwise be rather staid and lacking a vision can be transformed into shining examples of corporate communication that enable stakeholders to truly connect with the vision of the company.

—Vishal Dhawan[4]

Abstract

In this work, we have attempted to establish a link between the additional narrative of an annual report and the positioning that a company enjoys in the eyes of the public and the investors. The methodology followed is "différance," the pioneering work of Jacques Derrida used to arrive at subtextual persuasive framings in the annual reports. In the process, we unearthed significant differences in the surface narrative and certain alternative interpretations that emerge after "deconstruction." An effort is also made to hypothesize the usage of annual reports by companies as devices to allure prospective investors by matching the ideals of the investors with those of the company; the interpretive strategy-interpretive community framework of Stanley Fish has been an insightful lens of study for this purpose.

Introduction: Corporate Communication in the Industry

Corporate communication in the broad sense essentially means the sharing and transmission of information by people within an organization, primarily for its commercial benefit. Here emphasis is on the fact that it refers to the information transmitted by a company or corporation's own people, for it is their actions that define how a company is perceived in the public,

---

[4]Vishal Dhawan, Founder and CEO, Plan Ahead Wealth Advisors Pvt. Ltd.

media, and the investor's eyes. Whether the information is relayed through print, radio, television, or word of mouth, it is the primary avenue through which a company defines its marketing policies, molds public relations, and relates its financial status to its various stakeholders. It is easy to see why organizations would devote tremendous amounts of time highlighting their achievements and accomplishments and downplaying their shortcomings.

Corporate communication is goal oriented. The rules, regulations, and policies of a company have to be communicated to people within and outside the organization. Corporate communication is regulated by certain rules and norms. For example, annual reports have to conform to generally accepted accounting principles (GAAP) regulations for the reporting of financial figures. In earlier times, communication was limited to paper documents, telephone calls, and so on. But now with pervasiveness of technology, we have web-based communication, presentations, forums, discussion boards, and, of course, media reporting, which is largely outside of the company's control.

Annual Reports as Modes of Corporate Communication

Organizations today utilize several avenues for corporate communication that are not restricted to print media. However, by and large, the primary modus operandi that is uniformly accepted throughout remains in the form of annual reports. Published at the end of every financial year, they remain the go-to documents for any shareholder who has invested or who is interested in the company. By providing a comprehensive report about the company's previous activities, the annual report presents a detailed summary of the company's financials along with various other inputs such as a director's report, achievements of the past year, along with a vision for the coming year. Though usually prepared at great expense, many may not have a single investor read the entire document. Most of these reports often include a narrative that captures what the numbers cannot—intangibles such as patents, brands, and people. The annual report's structure and appearance can provide a lot of information on how the company views itself, not just in terms of numbers but as a collective account of how it is progressing. But while narratives can reflect wider changes going on within the company, nothing beats looking at the numbers. However, most retail investors lack the expertise to enable them to sift through a company's financials.

In the case of larger companies, the report is usually a cheerful, colorful, high-gloss publication, particularly with easy-to-read sections including the corporate social responsibility (CSR) section. As such, it should not come as a surprise that an annual report serves to present the company in best light possible without violating any norms and regulations. While many organizations are not required to produce an annual report, a wide range of not-for-profits—from associations to charities—choose to report on their accomplishments and promote financial transparency through an annual report.

Annual reports are an important tool for corporations to drive communication in a desired manner to all their stakeholders (present as well as prospective) as well as to the general public. The reports are a type of literature, so they are prepared with elaborate consideration to facilitate strategic audience response. These "elaborate considerations" then become core strategic facets of the writing or reading processes of corporate annual reports.

Key facets of annual reports generally include the following:

Targets for Annual Reports: The Stakeholders

- Investors (including institutional)
- Consumers via media
- Government and regulatory bodies
- Employees
- Competitors

Purposes of Annual Reports[5]

- Offers an opportunity to thank those who enable the company to fulfill their mission and makes the stakeholders feel part of the organization

---

[5]J. Winton. August, 2010. "4 reasons to publish an annual report this year," *Mission Minded 30*. http://mission-minded.com/4-reasons-to-publish-an-annual-report-this-year, (accessed April 13, 2018).

- Serves as a fundraising tool to help build relationships with investors
- Shares perspectives on the challenges of technology, conveys ideas about its role in the company, celebrates achievements, and articulates plans and visions for the future
- Relates human stories about the organization's work in the community and tries to justify its existence and value addition to society; also drives an emotional appeal about their work and develops rationale for their actions
- Provides a financial statement that includes the following four statements:
  - Balance sheet
  - Income statement
  - Statement of retained earnings
  - Statement of cash flow

These four statements are staples of any annual report. Over time, additional sections such as "letter to shareholders" and "messages from the board of directors" have also become a norm. Companies now face a growing competition for influencing people. As the single most widely read document about the company, the annual report provides a chance to anticipate how the company is perceived in light of trends and competitors and to articulate a forward-looking story about the company that reflects the vision and direction.[6] Companies need to create their own folklore. Folklore stories have survived through centuries because they communicate powerful stories that resonate with the readers. Usually, this folklore reinforces some ideal or set of values that transcend culture and customs. We can all think of companies with a story line or image that might well fit this description. Hence, it is no surprise that in the modern age, the persona of a company can be a powerful means to influence perception and reputation, and to buffer financial results.

---

[6]TRUE.creative services. 2014. *5 Reasons Why Your Organization Should Produce an Annual Report.* http://www.thisistruecs.com/2014/08/annual-reports-5-reasons, (accessed October 10, 2017).

Rivals and Threats to Annual Reports

- Media reports
- Social media campaigns
- Vigilante journalism such as WikiLeaks
- Independent studies
- Institutional investors' study
- Disclosure to regulators

Objective of Study

That annual reports are the face of corporations is a known fact. But considering annual reports as folklore that accentuates influence and thereby gathers strategic audience responses is a far more interesting addition to the understanding of corporate literature. In other words, annual reports "govern" the audience response through strategic writing or reading processes. It would be of pertinent research interest to understand the underlying "governance logic" of this strategic writing or reading anchors that annual reports use for productive persuasion and consumption. Since they are about writing or reading strategies, looking through annual reports with the aid of the Derridean *différance* lens is advantageous. The two primary characteristics of the *différance* tool of investigation are as follows:

- No text has absolute meaning.
- There is always some possibility of alternative interpretations because of the multilayered character of any text.

By reading annual reports, we take a deeper look into corporate communications and attempt a critical textual analysis. Doing so we aim to glean the notion of "truth" in these texts and try to assimilate alternative and contradictory meanings in select sections of these texts. Using Derrida's lens of *différance*, we will attempt to differentiate what is presented explicitly from its unstated yet underlying implication.

In order to study the conflicting subtexts in the annual reports, we were faced with the choice to either use the knowledge we have accrued as students of corporate finance to compare the companies and their explicitly advertised agendas that show themselves in good light or to dive deeper into the "unconscious subtextual linguistics" that reveal the anxieties of those very companies that are repositioned as strategic representations to external stakeholders. Derrida's work on *différance* enables us to do precisely the latter.

Analysis and Research Hypotheses

Data Used in the Analysis

We looked at 3 years of annual reports of two corporate giants—Infosys and Reliance—for a stipulated period of time—2012 to 2015—as starters to our analytical inquiry into extracting the subtleties of writing or reading annual reports, which are considered not just organizational reporting tools but strategic organizational "positioning" tools. In order to deconstruct the annual reports under study, we divided the texts into two parts: first, the financial reports, including the balance sheets or cash flow statements and their explanations, that are indicators of the financial performance of the company in the previous year; second, the additional narrative portion that usually forms the beginning of the report with "letters to shareholders," "message from the founding fathers," and descriptive accounts of the future strategy.

While applying the *différance* technique, we have considered only the second part of the reports of each of these organizations because these are the parts of the reports that vary from company to company; they are less data based and more narrative based, and hence more suitable to a folklore genre. The financial reports and their descriptors are same or along similar lines in all the six annual reports under study, due to GAAP requirements. As a consequence, we have consciously left out relevant financial analysis to arrive at our concept of a better positioning of the company via linguistic or narrative positioning.

Data Analysis: The Methodology

The following is the step-by-step process of how we performed an analysis on the additional narrative in the six annual reports.

1. We commenced by skimming the surface of the readings and determined the most important themes that stood out in the reports. These formed the research hypothesis (RH) discussed in the subsequent section.

2. We then dove deeper into the reports and tried to problematize "what was being claimed" by attempting alternative explanations for these claims. Here is where we used the deconstruction tool.
3. We emerged with final research propositions based on the preceding analysis.
4. We then validated our findings by applying them to the annual report of an external company not part of the original study.

Findings: Research Hypotheses

RH 1: *Having a changing theme for each annual report or having a constant theme year after year is equally important based on the strategy of organizational positioning.*

At the outset, what struck us while analyzing Infosys reports vis-à-vis Reliance is that the report of Infosys is a themed one whereas Reliance works with the company's basic tenet, year after year. Reliance works with the constant theme of "Growth is Life,"[7,8,9] whereas Infosys keeps altering the theme, year after year—for the 2012 report it was "Relevance through Innovation,"[10] for 2013 it was "Evolving with Changing Times,"[11] and 2014 saw the theme stylized as "Renew. New."[12]

The thematic positioning begs the question of the importance of publishing a themed report. Reliance with its single theme may be projecting consistence at the surface. Infosys may want to project itself as a dynamic organization with its rapidly shifting focus, with the theme acting as a proxy, probably to meet market demands.

However, our *différance* lens also allows us to prospect on the following dilemma: Is there a probability then that Reliance has its focus in 10 different directions simultaneously by tying the multiple focal points together under the forward-sounding umbrella of "Growth is Life"—that

[7]Reliance Industries Limited. 2013. "Growth is Life, Annual Report 2012-13," pp. i.
[8]Reliance Industries Limited. 2014. "Growth is Life, Annual Report 2013-14," pp. i.
[9]Reliance Industries Limited. 2015. "Growth is Life, Annual Report 2014-15," pp. i.
[10]Infosys. 2013. "Relevance through Innovation, Annual Report 2012-13," pp. i.
[11]Infosys. 2014. "Evolving with Changing Times, Annual Report 2013-14," pp. i.
[12]Infosys. 2015. "Renew. New. Annual Report 2014-15," pp. i.

life may be spreading thin is not something the investors would care to think about? Similarly, for Infosys, the subtextual premise may be that while being dynamic is important for survival, changing focus every year might also point to the fact that the upper management is *prospecting* on what is working through contextual evaluation than standardized followership.

> **RH 2**: *The additional narrative in the report acts as a proxy for future strategy.*

We must understand that the financial statements and the numbers they convey are the most important part of any annual report. However, the numbers alone cannot form a sufficient tool for conveying information. The financial statements represent the performance of the company in the past one year. The numbers do not and cannot convey what the leadership of the firm has in store for the future—short term and long term as well. This is where the role of the additional narrative comes into play. Using amplified statements as well as a healthy dose of buzzwords, a company can convey the strategy that it will follow—whether it is breaking from the previous norms of self or industry, or becoming aligned with industry best practices. Consider the following excerpt:

> In September 2012, Forbes ranked us among the 19 most innovative companies in the world. This recognition only makes us more aware of our responsibilities, more committed to finding avenues for innovation [. . .], and more interested in doing things differently.[13]

[Infosys Annual Report 2012–2013]

Infosys of 2012 to 2013 is a "company of relentless innovators on a mission."[14] With the 2012 to 2013 annual report entirely focusing on innovating and how it has been the driving force forever for the company, one is lulled into thinking that the main focus of the company is to innovate.

---

[13]Infosys. 2013. "Relevance through Innovation, Annual Report 2012-13," pp. v.

[14]Infosys. 2013. "Relevance through Innovation, Annual report 2012-13," pp. iii.

The "truth" can be polyvalent. We believe that just like any other company, profit is what drives the company. In order to stay profitable and ahead in their industry, the company can either compete head on with other firms in the same area or they can look for untapped opportunities, as they claim to "go about building tomorrow's markets"[15] and innovate solutions for them. Appearing progressive, then, seems to be the "anxious" strategy.

Consider this instance:

RIL is striving to meet and exceed global benchmarks in product quality and customer service with inspiring ideas and strategic investments.[16]

[RIL Annual Report 2014–2015]

The Reliance (RIL) quote is a statement that clearly communicates to any reader of the report that RIL is conforming to international best practices, an attractive signal to a risk-averse investor. On the other hand, look at the following:

We have constantly endeavored to operate at the forefront of new technologies. We have invested in continuously developing new products and seeking new applications, which are suitable for Indian markets and conditions.[17]

[RIL Annual report 2012–2013]

Here the statement is trying to focus on innovations and disruptions, and trying to break the industry norms—a move well calculated to cater to a risky investor's fancy. (But if the guy is investing in an established firm, instead of a really new startup, he's not much of a risk-taker, is he?)

RH 3: *It is important for the companies to sound and look socially responsible.*

---

[15]Reliance Industries Limited. 2015. "Growth is Life, Annual Report 2014-15," pp. ii.
[16]Reliance Industries Limited. 2013. "Growth is Life, Annual Report 2012-13," pp. ii.
[17]Reliance Industries Limited. 2015. "Growth is Life, Annual Report 2014-15," pp. 32.

For all companies today, there exists an increasing emphasis to project themselves as socially responsible, with the "triple bottom line" being the newer, more acceptable form of the traditional bottom line, which was driven solely by profits and profitability. And while it matters that a company does actual work towards the triple bottom line, it is equally important that it highlights its efforts and that its annual reports present an excellent opportunity to entice the socially responsible investor.

We attempted to find out if, in reality, the narrative of the annual report is being used to forward the socially responsible angle of the company. To this end, we used a simple word counting filter, summarized in Table 2.1, to find out how many times certain "buzzwords" are used in the texts of the reports.

Table 2.1 Recurring buzzwords on social responsibility in reports

Keyword/report	Infosys $12–13^{12}$	Infosys $13–14^{13}$	Infosys $14–15^{14}$	RIL $12–13^9$	RIL $13–14^{10}$	RIL $14–15^{11}$
Innovation	76	43	55	149	46	70
Innovative	22	10	25	10	10	22
Sustainable	13	25	18	17	27	38
Environmental	20	34	21	40	57	61
Growth	45	93	67	320	571	406
Social	31	59	54	26	70	144
Profit	177	226	262	125	168	180

It is evident that all the annual reports we studied were liberally peppered with words such as "innovation," "innovative," "sustainable," and "environmental." While all these words appear on the annual reports of both companies, what is even more important to notice is that the number of times a word is mentioned is showing disparate trends in the companies under study. Reliance shows a clear growth year after year in the number of times it mentions the words; Infosys depicts a *peaking* form, that is, the number goes up and then comes down, indicating a clear change in positioning or strategy between the years 2013 and 2015. What that change was remains to be seen.

An even more striking issue is the fact that even though the buzzwords are present in abundance, typical corporate words such as "growth" and "profit" are even more present (a trend more visible in Reliance than Infosys), given their recurring numbers. Also, the words such as "profit" and "profitability" are noticeably absent from the initiating narratives in the reports, even though their numbers prove their importance to the company. This absence indicates that building interest of the forward-thinking investor through forward-thinking strategy can and is being done through the narrative, but the subtextual and the main motive still remains profit, which is skillfully understated using the "cool" words of the time.

RH 4: *The order in which items are covered in the annual report may seem unimportant, but it can act as proxy for the priorities of the company.*

A major difference between Reliance and Infosys is the order in which they report same or similar items in the annual reports. A case in point is the order in which the "Awards and Recognition" section has presented. For Infosys, the Awards and Recognition section forms a subsection under the Director's Report. Reliance has this as a main section in the additional narrative and in the form of an infographic. This might seem a small difference; but through *différance* logic, this is also done with a strategy in mind. While in Infosys, the sections might even get overlooked when an investor is skimming through the report, for Reliance, this section is a major eye-catcher using the strategy of appearing best in the field.

RH 5: *The complexity of the narrative acts as a barrier to the investor.*

Corporate documents are by design, increasingly dense and dull. The narrative of the annual report is one in which familiar words are used in unfamiliar ways. For example, the term "gross" meaning in totality and "profit" when combined to form "gross profit" in an annual report, in essence means that some prior knowledge is needed to understand what precisely the new term means. Even with a basic course in financial analysis, many a reader will find it difficult to decode what is being said in the narrative or in the core financial statements. It is understood that the reports are a way of letting the common investor make an informed decision while deciding whether to invest or not, or to revalue his or her prior investments in the company stocks. However, the report is full of jargon and with no key to decode it. The investor may oftentimes be left hanging and may not be able to arrive at the investment decision alone.

The difficulty in reading annual reports points to a complicit move on the part of the reporting company to erect a barrier for the common investor so that she or he has to solicit help from brokers, further providing fuel for another thriving industry. Even professionals are frustrated with the process of deconstructing the reports. Consider the case of Andrew, an individual investor, who was found tossing heaps of unopened annual reports into a recycling bin in his city:

> "Every year it's [the annual reports] the same," Andrew said. "I mean to read the annual reports and proxies but I don't have the time and I don't really know what to look for, and my broker is satisfied with what I own and would tell me if he felt we needed to make changes. [. . .] At some point, there's this big stack of paperwork cluttering up the house and I'm busy and I don't want to look at it anymore, so I just throw it all out. . . . I'd feel horrible if anything went really wrong with a stock, but it hasn't happened yet."[18]

RH 6: *The annual report is as much a tool for effective marketing as it is for financial reporting.*

The trend of annual reports that are all text has long passed. All the reports we analyzed were of the new era—text-y yet replete with splashes of color and interesting graphics.

Pick any report under study and you will find yourself facing collages of founding fathers, engaged board of directors, happy employees, and smiling stakeholders, along with images from industries, plants, and other assets of the organization. The thought that crosses the mind then is whether these reports are intended solely for the purpose of financial reporting or are they also being used as marketing devices to catch and

---

[18]C. Jaffe. April 7, 2014. "4 Things Smart Investors Look for in Annual Reports," http://www.marketwatch.com/story/4-things-to-look-for-in-annual-reports-2014-04-04, (accessed April 2, 2018).

hold shareholder attention. Also, if the attention getting goal happens to be true, the further question is whether this strategy of marketing the company through the report is really effective. Consider an amateur looking to make investments, and the only way she or he is going to make the decision of where to invest will be based on reading of annual reports. Going through a report, she or he would want to invest in the one that is able to back up its narrative with exciting images. Now consider an institutional investment decision, or a serious individual investor. It seems hardly likely that the investment decision in this case will be swayed by anything short of the numbers emerging from the financial statements.

On this train of thought, the question arises of who exactly is being targeted through these annual reports in the first place—the serious investor who is likely to make a larger sum of investments, or the easily swayed common investors whose investments may be small?

While looking at the annual reports in hand, we arrive at a stark contrast between the two giants; and that is, the Reliance reports contain more images of employees and stakeholders through the Reliance Foundation section of the report. Infosys reports also contain images, but they are few and far in between and are also mostly of the upper echelon of the company such as the Board members. This could mean that Reliance wants to be the picture of a people's company, emphasizing the number of lives they touch through their vast portfolio, whereas this may not be a key focus for Infosys, which mainly engages with corporate partners and not directly with the common Indian.

Findings: Corporate Propositions

Summarizing the research hypotheses in the previous section, we have established the following corporate propositions (CPs) that have been derived from recurring textual positionings in the annual reports under consideration:

- CP1: The theme of an annual report can be seen as a sign of focus or a show of dynamism and can act in favor of the organization if the theme is backed by appropriate actions in the past and current years.

- CP2: While the narrative is an additional part of the annual report, it is important in conveying strategy in ways that cannot be accomplished solely based on the financial numbers.
- CP3: To remain competitive, it is important to project the firm as socially responsible and/or aligned with any new "happening" movement.
- CP4: The order of reporting shows the priorities of the firm, if you dig deep enough.
- CP5: The narrative of the report is purposely difficult to comprehend by an amateur stakeholder and hence acts to support the flourishing broker industry.
- CP6: Indeed, annual reports fulfill a dual purpose—financial reporting as well as marketing.

Application of CPs in Developing Annual Reports

We applied the findings from our RHs to an organization external to this study. For this purpose we selected Marico,[19] which is a major Indian fast-moving consumer goods (FMCG) company with products including Parachute and Saffola. Here is what we found out when aligning Marico report with our CPs:

- Application of CP1: Marico employs a yearly theme for reporting purposes. While the reason may be different from Infosys, but the intention may remain the same, that of projecting dynamism.
- Application of CP2: The additional narrative is plenty, and far more graphic than the report of either Reliance or Infosys. However, the report does not depict any photographs of board of directors (BoDs), the founding fathers, or stakeholders. The dominant images present are those of the products. This may be attributed to the fact that Marico is an FMCG company and its core strength is its brands, which it may want to project in the best light.
- Application of CP3: As far as appearance of social responsibility and related buzzwords go, it should be enough to say that the first

---

[19]Marico. 2015. "Transforming Marico, Annual Report 2014–15."

word of the additional narrative in the report in question is "Inno-vation." Look at Marico's progressive use of buzzwords in Table 2.2 through 2012 to 2013, 2013 to 2014, and 2014 to 2015.

Table 2.2 Recurring buzzwords on social responsibility in Marico annual reports

Marico	2012–2013	2013–2014	2014–2015
Innovation	20	60	78
Innovate	0	5	8
Sustainable	2	13	23
Environmental	1	2	8
Growth	65	189	280
Social	2	30	73
Profit	143	189	161

- Application of CP4: As mentioned in application of CP2, the FMCG giant is very clearly using the report to promote its activi-ties and products.
- Application of CP5: The body of the report here also is full of jargon, which puts it in the same class as almost all other annual reports subjected to GAAP regulations.
- Application of CP6: As mentioned in application of CP2, the FMCG giant is very clearly using the report to market its activities and products.

Findings: The Governance Logic of Corporate Annual Reports

Based on the discussion culled from Infosys, Reliance, and Marico, we extract the following tenet of what governs the strategic positioning of an organization through an annual report. The Derridean *différance* model of meaning production is produced from the difference (to differ) in positioning created by the representation of the leadership (as in Infosys) versus the common people (as in Reliance, where it's the employees in the pictures) versus the products (as in Marico), and the futuristic growth they refer to as in the contextual deference for Infosys (we will meet the current requirement types) and a grand narrative of growth for Reliance (we will meet the grand requirement types). However, both the "difference" and "deference" have a stamp of credibility, and it is this basic framing of the *différance* in annual reports that generates the stakeholder (investor) trust.

Final Corporate Proposition: This governing principle of the annual report is a technique by which the profit-generation motive of the organization is made acceptable through a style of narration that appeals to the investor's ideals.

Explanation of the Final CP

Legitimization is done by employing complex jargons and formulae as well as broad based catchy phrases such as "innovation" and "sustainability." This helps top managers to keep their ivory towers intact. The complexity of these reports is done by the same class of people who are driven by more or less similar agenda. These complex terms act as entry barriers for individual stakeholders to "read between the lines." Moreover, shareholders designate top managers to look after the company; and due to a complex functioning structure of the company, there is information asymmetry. Annual reports are tools of corporate communication to stakeholders. But how stakeholders interpret these tools, is again up to these top managers. Annual reports are woven around core value propositions that would attract respective stakeholders. In other words, what investors would fall for is already embedded into the textual life of the organization core values. On the other hand, annual reports have to conform to certain standards such as GAAP, which in itself, let alone its content, is a term alien to common people. Hence, in some way the top management justifies their contribution and existence along with the huge perks they take home.

Furthermore, there is a conscious effort to balance between profit driven and social motive. The rationale for corporate management decisions is justified by creating a narrative—a mix of scintillating numbers, stories of impact, cheerful pictures, and most importantly, framing the deferred capital of "hopes": hope for a better future. Consider another instance of deference framed as deferred capital: Balance sheet emphasis on innovation and sustainability overlooks other failures, particularly in corporate responsibility. Profits can mean demand for higher dividend by shareholders, lower prices by consumers, negation of tax breaks if not higher taxes by government, and better prices to suppliers. Hence, corporations underplay profits behind the loud framing of investment needed to build the country's infrastructure that shall help generate employment and help consumers with better products (grand deference plans). Also, shareholders are told of the necessity to invest in innovation to stay ahead of the "learning curve." "Investing in innovation" is what would bring the *difference* in identity, and this *difference* would *eventually lead to* "staying ahead in the game," something that has *yet to happen*, but *would happen* if aligned with the industry best practices (the necessary *deference*). So the legitimization of profit is produced through the following steps:

- Alignment with current industry practices in vogue (or larger good practices always in vogue) and hence have a *distinctive* existence (difference).
- Alignment that would necessarily imply that the stakeholder would *eventually* reach a position of profit (deference).

The end result of these subtextual maneuvers in annual reports is the legitimization of profit, as well as the establishment of credibility for the organization and stakeholder trust.

Epilogue[20]

Stanley Fish and his notion of the interpretive community are very insightful in estimating the contribution of the authors on the governance logic of the *différance* model in the framing of organizational positionings in annual reports. Now, let us rewrite the *différance* grammar of the annual reports again.

So the legitimization of profit is produced through the following means:

- Alignment with current industry practices in vogue (or larger good practices always in vogue). This entails that there is a desired interpretive community that would have readers who would interpret

---

[20]Contributed by Pragyan Rath, Communications, Indian Institute of Management Calcutta.

the text, and the annual reports have to get those readers interpret (read) the text in a desired fashion (very pro-organization of course). To do so, the writers already have prior knowledge on those *aspirations of differences* (already existing, thanks to prior norms and prior cultural inductions) in the subcultural sentiments of the readers, and also further architect *aspirations of differences* in the subcultural premises of these readers that perpetuate at a visible level defining clearly "what is in there for the stakeholder" but at a subtextual level also takes care of their own organizational intentions.

- Alignment would necessarily imply that the stakeholder would eventually reach a position of profit. The *aspirations of differences* are interpreted as much as what would eventually be the consequence of these *differences*; hence, the *aspirations of deference* (that which will be, is not yet) is a further necessary "interpretive strategy"—a Stanley Fish coinage again.

So, what we can further cull on the governance logic that administers the writing of annual reports is the inevitable authority on interpretations through developments of reading and writing parameters we can reframe as the *interpretive annual report reading or writing communities*. The stark question by Fish plays out well here: "Why will different readers execute the same interpretive strategy when faced with the 'same' text?"[21] He says that it does not need to be so. But we superimpose the CPs contributed by the authors to what Fish offers:

> [Organizational] [i]nterpretive communities are made up of those [stakeholders] who share interpretive strategies not for reading (in the conventional sense) but for writing texts [annual reports], for constituting their properties and assigning their intentions [as the authors have established in their CPs]. In other words, these strategies [RHs and CPs] exist prior to the act of reading and therefore determine the shape of what is read [performative] rather than, as is usually assumed,

---

[21]S. Fish. "'Interpretive Communities.' From '"Interpreting the Variorum."'" In *The Norton Anthology of Theory & Criticism*. 2nd ed., eds. V. B. Leitch and W. W. Cain. New York, NY: Norton, 1974–1992 (1988–1992). pp. 1990–1991.

the other way around. If it is an article of faith in a particular community that there are a variety of texts, its members will boast a repertoire of strategies for making them. And if a community believes in the existence of only one text, then the single strategy its members employ will be forever writing it. [. . .] The assumption in each community will be that the other is not correctly perceiving the "true text," but the truth will be that each perceives the text (or texts) its interpretive strategies demand and call into being. This, then, is the explanation both for the stability of interpretation among different readers (they belong to the same community) and for the regularity with which a single reader will employ different interpretive strategies and thus make different texts ([s/he] belongs to different communities).[22]

So, let us look at the possibility of the identification of the interpretive strategies that demand and call into being the meaning of each text from the formation of the corporate annual report reading or writing interpretive community developed from and by us in our contribution to developing a definable governance logic for writing corporate annual reports. Let us reinterpret the governance logic positionings of the CPs culled by us when discussing the annual reports of the two information technology (IT) giants. We have made heavy generalizations of subtextual interpretations to develop reference points of an imagined corporate annual report readership interpretive community. Table 2.3 delineates these generic interpretive positionings.

So what we can get from a contrasting study of reading or writing interpretive strategies of the two industry giants is the following clustering of narrative type, positioning type, and the investor (stakeholder/audience) type.

The six CPs and their narrative, strategy, and investor connections are as follows:

- The theme (CP1) can either be constant or dynamic. For constant theme, the interpreter is conservative and hence will be a communal investor. For dynamic theme, the interpreter is prospecting in attitude and will be a contextual investor.

---

[22]Ibid.

Table 2.3 Strategic framings for corporate annual report writership/ readership interpretive community

Reliance positioning from CPs	Generic reference positioning	Infosys positioning from corporate propositions	Generic reference positioning
CP1: Theme: CONSTANT *What properties to look for* • Focused but dynamic underneath • Mission–Vision statements • Tying multifaceted goals into one outlook • Defocus on changing contexts (difference is more prominent by being part of grand narratives)	Writer: *Conservative* Communicator Reader: Demanding and calling into being of a risk-averse (communal) investor/reader	CP1: Theme: DYNAMIC *What properties to look for* • Evolving with changing times (focus about context than aim) • Defocus on output • Make context more evident (deference is more prominent)	Writer: *Prospecting* Communicator Reader: Demanding and calling into being of a risk-taking (contextual) investor/reader
CP2: Strategy: CONFORMIST *What properties to look for* • Meet benchmarks: "aligned with international best practices" (difference is more prominent by being part of elite clubs and practices)	Writer: *Cult* Communicator Reader: Demanding and calling into being of a risk-averse (communal) investor/reader	CP2: Strategy: FUTURISTIC *What properties to look for* • Buzzwords: "innovation," "tomorrow's markets" • Defocus current scenario and stress on future contexts (deference is more prominent)	Writer: *Leadership* Communicator Reader: Demanding and calling into being of a risk-taking (contextual) investor/reader
CP3: Social responsibility: ADD-ONS *What properties to look for* • Keeps adding buzzwords • Abiding with add-ons (difference is more prominent by being part of grand narratives)	Writer: *Cumulative* Positioning Reader: Demanding and calling into being of a risk-averse (communal) investor/reader	CP3: Social Responsibility: CONTEXTUAL *What properties to look for* • Changes with context • Futuristic in what is current and that is their aim (deference is more prominent)	Writer: *Peaking* Positioning Reader: Demanding and calling into being of a risk-taking (contextual) investor/reader

(continued)

Table 2.3 (Continued)

CP4: Prioritizing: MEMBERSHIP *What properties to look for* • Awards and recognitions as distinct mentions (difference is more prominent by being part of elite clubs and practices)	Writer: *Clustering* Reader: Demanding and calling into being of a risk-averse (communal) investor/reader	CP4: Prioritizing: MOVEMENTS *What properties to look for* • Awards and recognitions as subsets of leadership council/cluster interviews, speeches, discourse	Writer: *Performing* Reader: Demanding and calling into being of a risk-taking (contextual) investor/reader
CP5: Linguistic complexity: DENSE *What properties to look for* • GAAP norms • Due visibility of simple visuals of stakeholders as well	Writer: *Alignment* Reader: alliance to cult/brokerage	CP5: Linguistic Complexity: DENSER *What properties to look for* • GAAP norms • Denser language and finance	Writer: *Partnership* Reader: Demanding and calling into corollary readership (brokerage)
CP6: Purpose: MARKETING *What properties to look for* • People's company: rhetoric of stakeholders (visuals of employees as mainstay) • Customer-centric	Writer: **Service** Reader: Demanding and calling into being of a risk-averse (communal) investor/reader	CP6: Purpose: STRATEGY *What properties to look for* • Strategy angle more strong • Speeches of Leaders hold main space • Denser linguistic complexity • Advocating future missions • Presenting alliances with future leaders	Writer: **Trend** Reader: Demanding and calling into being of a risk-taking (contextual) investor/reader

• The strategy (CP2) can be a conformist or a futuristic one. For a conformist strategy, the investor will have propensity for cult, and will therefore be a communal investor. For the futuristic strategy, the investor with have propensity for leadership and thus will be more of a contextual investor.

- For social responsibility anchors (CP3), the reports may have heavy add-ons, or contextual buzzwords. Add-ons each year will be favored by communal investors looking for cumulative additions, while contextual buzzwords attract contextual investors interested in peaking forms.
- The narrative prioritizing (CP4) may, through membership narratives attract communal investors looking for clustering, while narratives of movements will attract contextual investors looking for performances rather than clusters.
- The linguistic density (CP5) that defines parameters of alignment attracts conservative investors, while listing partnership clauses will attract contextual investors.
- The purpose (CP6) projected as marketing will gather service-oriented conservative investors, while purpose projecting strategy will gather trend-directed contextual investors.

In other words, the CPs derived may be reframed as strategic points of interpretation in the writing of corporate annual reports, as represented in a generalized diagrammatic form in Figure 2.1. The interesting angle in this psychodynamic relation amidst these various proponents of reports is the set of combinations and permutations that can be interpreted to develop more complex psychodynamic connectors.

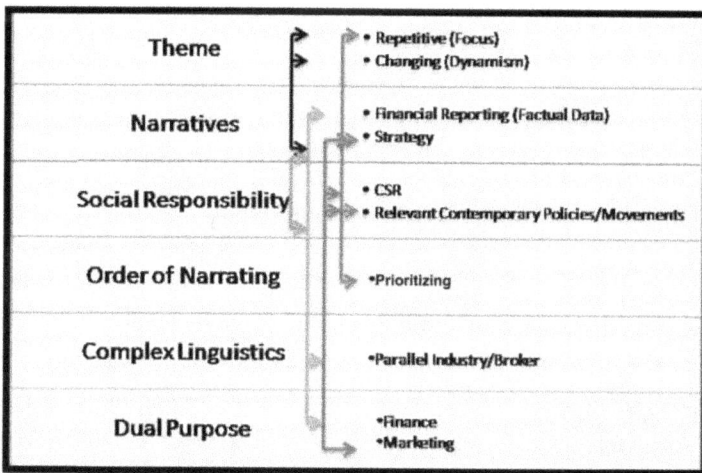

Figure 2.1 *Interpretive strategies for writing corporate annual reports*

Let us connect our CPs with the Strategic Framings. The theme (CP1) and the narrative (CP2) may be interconnected for strategic interpretations as represented by the corresponding connector in Figure 1. So an organization might position itself as dynamic (thematically) while into heavy financial reporting; or could be more focused "thematically" while into heavy financial reporting, or could have a more "strategy-driven" narration though remaining focused on its grand narrative "theme." One can try different permutations and combinations with CP1 and CP2. Similarly, from the same figure, we can derive another set of permutations and combinations amidst narratives (CP2), linguistic complexities (CP5), and purpose (CP6). For instance, the organization may be heavily into strategy, but more financial data advocacy would imply good partnership with the broker industry and yet have a more marketing appeal than present a more financial reporting style. Look at the other possible permutations and combinations amidst CP2 and CP3 with their corresponding connector; CP2, CP3, and CP6 (corresponding connector marked); CP1, CP2, CP3, and CP4 (corresponding connector marked). Thus, we get myriad structures of Interpretive Strategies and their corresponding complex Interpretive Communities.

Research Takeaways

Application of Interpretive Strategies and Interpretive Communities in decoding the Intent and the Outcome of the Annual Reports Narratives.

From Table 2.3 and Figure 2.1, we actually produce a framework for a matrix of correspondence between Interpretive Strategies and Interpretive Communities. The more the number of strategic interpretive frames/points, the more number of clusters or subclusters of interpretive communities can be developed. Due to the limited audition of data starters, we have developed here the basic Annual Report Interpretive Matrix of Strategies and Communities, which within the limitation of the data set studied helps develop a hexagonal matrix with six interpretive strategic points of reference (the six CPs). The midpoints of each axis would be the permutation/combination interpretive strategic reference points. Table 2.4 shows the six CPs and the six midpoint interpretive strategic frames for writing or reading annual reports.

Now, if we convert Table 2.4 into a hexagon and chart the interpretive communities of any organization under their broad interpretive strategic points, midpoints, and submidpoints identified from their annual reporting narrative reading, we can have an area diagram within the hexagon that would actually

Table 2.4 Points, midpoints, and submidpoints of interpretive strategic frames for wring/reading annual report hexagon

CP points	Midpoints	Submidpoints
Theme (CP1)	PL (prospecting leadership)	
Strategy (CP2)		PL-CC
Strategy (CP2)	CC (cult–cumulative)	
Social responsibility (CP3)		CC-PP
Social responsibility (CP3)	PP (peaking–performing)	
Priority (CP4)		PP-CA
Priority (CP4)	CA (clustering–alignment)	
Linguistic complexity (CP5)		CA-PT
Linguistic complexity (CP5)	PT (partnership–trend)	
Purpose (CP6)		PT-SC

plot the interpretive community designed and demanded by the organization that has plotted these interpretive strategic framings in the textual nature of their annual reports. The area deciphered is the desired or intended interpretive cluster of the "prospective" investor, shareholder, stakeholder, stockholder, and other members of the community, as illustrated in Figure 2.2.

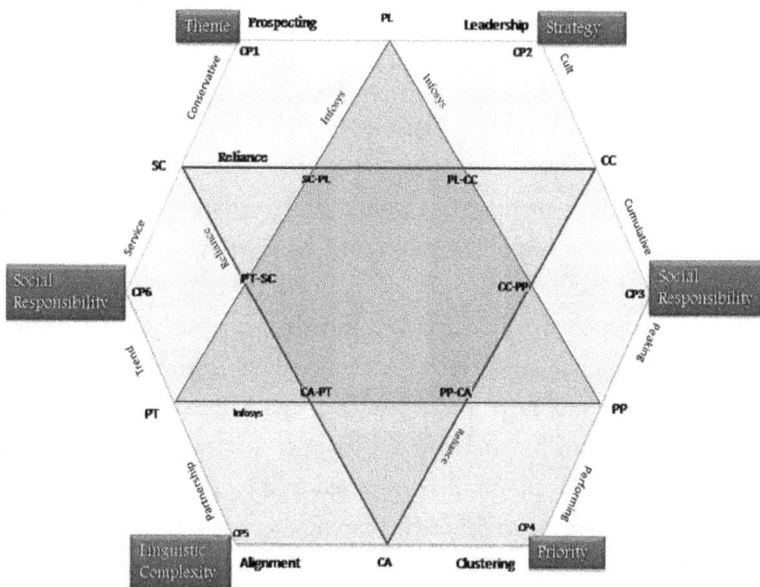

Figure 2.2 Interpretive communities of organizations designed in annual reports

Future Applications

Let us reinterpret Figure 2.2. The CP points are the broader strategic interpretive axes that are perhaps easily decipherable to a reading community. They catch the attention of the investor, and are meant to. The midpoints on those axes are the more intricate permutations and combinations of CPs, and they form the "hidden" cues to gather the *instinctive* investor—lead them to the organization. The submidpoints are perhaps the inevitable common ground or the collective judgment of the larger community, who could go either way—the prospecting organization or the conservative organization. Hence, the submidpoint interpretive strategies of framing in annual reports are inevitable statements ready-made for and directed to the basic population who would be reading annual reports. The *différance* creating interpretive strategy, however, lies in developing the midpoint interpretive strategies—they are the clues, cues, instinctual, subtextual, leading incentives for the desired reader/interpreter, and thereby the strategic persuasion parameters for constructing the annual reports.

For instance, for Reliance, in the current hexagon, there are three possible codes for developing interpretive communities, as depicted in Figure 2.2.

- **Possibility 1**: The persuasive area for actual strategic leading would be within the triangular points of SC (service–conservative), SC-PL (service–conservative/prospecting–leadership), and PT-SC (partnership–trend/service–conservative). Thus, while a fair sprinkling of the leadership values will be either evident for a more prospecting proposition with partnership and trend properties (heavy broker dependent with awards mentioned by Leadership Council), the conservative anchoring will be sustained through recurring motifs of service properties and conservative thematics (overall growth and heavy employee-centric visuals). Hence, the *communal* investor will be attracted to the organization despite a good dimension of futuristic framings.
- **Possibility 2**: The CC, PL-CC, and CC-PP triangle leads the *communal* investor to bet on Reliance. Cult and cumulative framing

(part of industry best practices and a plethora of buzzwords as add-ons) will outshine the red herrings in prospecting–leadership properties (Leadership Council promoting contextual futures) and peaking–performing properties (current buzzword along with futuristic activities).

- **Possibility 3**: The CA, CA-PT, and PP-CA area anchors Reliance persuasion. Clustering–alignment (industry best practices) will lead the persuasion cues amidst partnership–trend (dense linguistics but futuristic evaluations) and peaking–performing properties (current buzzword and futuristic activities).

Now, let us interpret the Infosys persuasion strategy in its three possible strategic framings as well, as depicted in Figure 2.2:

- **Possibility 1**: PL, PL-CC, and SC-PL
- **Possibility 2**: PP, PP-CA, and CC-PP
- **Possibility 3**: PT, PT-SC, and CA-PT

We can analyze organizational annual reports within these hexagonal structures to establish the stock market interpreter. Given an ample set of data and the drawing of a more detailed framing structure, we can understand how to attract the desired or intended interpreter (investor, shareholder, stakeholder, employee, and other varieties of corporate interpreters) by just studying the strategies used to develop the organizational interpretive community.

CHAPTER 3

The Poirot Way

K. Shalini[1]

Review Speak

Consumption habits of consumers worldwide are changing rapidly over time. It is increasingly becoming more important to understand consumers better—not only what they consume and how they consume but also their fundamental belief systems, how beliefs shape their attitudes, and how these attitudes in turn drive their purchase decisions and consumption behavior. The depth to which a researcher can go (in terms of understanding) depends a lot on the type of data and the quality of available data. Hence, one of the key priorities for the market research industry today is identifying how to capture data more effectively from consumers.

—Dhrubojyoti Sinha[2]

Abstract

In the age and times of cutthroat competition, it is imperative to understand your consumers and provide them with what they want. To achieve this, organizations use various investigative tools to do market research. One of the most difficult aspects of market research

(continued)

[1]K. Shalini, Probationary Officer, State Bank of India (SBI).
[2]Dhrubojyoti Sinha, Associate Vice President, Kantar IMR.B.

is how to elicit information from different kinds and types of con-sumers—let us call them "contextual consumers." In this chapter, we provide a new investigative tool termed "the HP code" derived from the legendary Hercule Poirot series of Agatha Christie and the conver-sation patterns of the little detective. This tool can be used to gather more accurate and relevant information by developing a contextual mechanism to understand and respond to an "implied reader," and thereby develop and establish the codes of communication of an inter-pretive community.

"In conversation, points arise! If a human being converses much, it is impossible for him to avoid the truth!"[3]

Once upon a time . . . in a far, far away land . . .

Stories—a source of entertainment and also a source of information dis-semination. Stories deliver information, sometimes real and sometimes fictional. They deliver the psyche of the writer and the reader, their thoughts and their opinions. They become a source of amusement and also a bundle of knowledge. What make the stories palatable are the char-acters and the narrations. When the characters in the fiction are coherent with the tastes of the reader, they instigate a different story within the reader. One such character who knew how to respond and how to elicit information is Hercule Poirot.

As created by Agatha Christie, Hercule Poirot was,

an extraordinary looking little man. He was hardly more than five feet, four inches, but carried himself with great dignity. His head was exactly the shape of an egg . . . His moustache was very stiff and military. The neatness of his attire was almost incredible.[4]

---

[3]A. Christie. n.d. "Hercule Poirot's Christmas." *Goodreads*. https://www.goodreads.com/quotes/434883-in-conversation-points-arise-if-a-human-being-converses-much, (accessed November 26, 2018)

[4]A. Christie. August 29, 2018. *The Mysterious Affair at Styles*. Quoted in *Poirot: The Life and Times of Hercule Poirot* by Anne Hart. pp. 18. HarperCollins. London. 1997. https://www.pagebypagebooks.com/Agatha_Christie/The_Mysterious_Affair_at_Styles/II_The_16th_And_17th_Of_July_p3.html

Hercule Poirot was a quaint, dandified, and debatably subtle detective who walked the streets of London and who conversed with people and exposed murderers. Poirot was a man who understood that it is important to take in both truths and lies equally, as it is during the course of conversations that people are given to inevitable slips regardless of an otherwise tight plan. So, what do we have here?

In this chapter, we study the conversation patterns of Hercule Poirot in relation to the characters with which he engaged. The endeavor here is to develop a model of communication, with the help of Poirot conversations, to extract information.

Personality Layout: The HP (Hercule Poirot) Code

We will first consider the various personality types that occur in the series. We have divided them on the basis of the character's life stages and current sub-stations. We then further differentiate between them with their dominant characteristics and the proclivity they show towards the positive or negative sides of a characteristic/attribute. This process results in the following HP code:

The HP code = (Life stage + Sub-station)
×(Dominant Characteristic + Proclivity)

Let us take a look, in Tables 3.1 and 3.2, at the character and sub-station divisions extracted from the Poirot series so that we can further understand the nomenclature process of the codes attributed to different characters.

Life stages have been broadly classified into eight categories, and each of them has specific stations particular to that life stage—for instance, a person who is single and adult might either be looking for a partner or is content with singlehood. Ten dominant characteristics have been identified as per the characters present in the Poirot series, including work style, pride, intellect, and others.

We look at the formula bar again and try to codify a few characters.

The HP Code = (Life stage + Sub-station)
×(Dominant Characteristic + Proclivity)

Table 3.1 The HP code: Life stages and sub-stations

1. Children/Students a. Lives with parent(s)/guardian/provider b. Does not live with parent(s)/guardian/provider	**2. Single Adults** a. Looking for a companion b. Content with living a single life

3. Married
a. Spouses devoted to each other
b. One of the couples devoted
c. Loveless marriage
	4. Married with Children
	a. Children living with parents
	b. Children living separate from parents
	
	  i. Loves kids but not the spouse
	  ii. Loves the spouse but not kids
	  iii. Loves the family
	  iv. Loves none in the family

5. Married with adult children who no longer live with parents a. Loves kids but not the spouse b. Loves the spouse but not kids c. Loves the family d. Loves none in the family	**6. Divorced without children** a. Living alone b. Remarried/engaged/cohabitating
7. Divorced with children a. Living alone b. Remarried/engaged (Living with spouse only) c. Living with children and the spouse d. Living without children e. Living with children	**8. Widow/Widower** a. Lone survivor b. Remarried/engaged /cohabitating c. Living with children

Evelyn Howard of *The Mysterious Affair at Styles* was identified as a young lady who is efficient at her work and is compassionate. Further developments in the story tell us that she would like to be engaged or married. The HP code for such a person would be 2.(ii).C.Efficient.b. Thus, "2" is her life stage, "(ii)" is the sub-station, "C" is her work style and her dominant characteristic, and her proclivity is Efficient, where (b) further denotes her positive inclination as generosity.

Charles Cartwright of *Three Act Tragedy* was the outstanding actor who loved to act a part on and off the stage. A man much older than the girl whom he loved despite being secretly married, he was charming

Table 3.2 The HP code: Dominant characteristics and proclivity

A. Success (in terms of money)	• **Well-off**
	• **Bad-off**
	  • a. Devoted to the provider
	  • b. Not devoted to the provider

B. Intellect	• **Imaginative** • **Non-imaginative**

C. Work style	• **Efficient**
	  • a. Malicious
	  • b. Remains generous
	• **Clumsy**
	  • a. Malicious
	  • b. Remains generous

D. Appeal to the opposite sex	• **Charming**
	  • a. Pure intentions
	  • b. Evil intentions
	• **Non-charmer**
	  • a. Loves deeply
	  • b. Aloof and evil

E. Resolution	• **Resolute** • **Nervous**
F. Humor and wit	• **Humorous** • **Non-humorous**
G. Pride	• **Proud** • **Humble**
H. Impression on audience	• **Flattering** • **Consumed**
I. Commitment to work	• **Engrossed** • **Not committed**
J. Temperament	• **Short tempered** • **Calm**

to everyone who had the opportunity to talk to him. The HP code for Mr. Cartwright is 3.(iii).D.Charming.b. The "3" denotes his married status, while "(iii)" is the sub-station that designates his loveless marriage. His appeal to the opposite sex as a man of outstanding charm becomes his dominant characteristic signified by "D." "Charming. b" points towards his charming persona while indicating an evil side to it.

Data Collection

We have projected the conversation style that detective Poirot chose while talking to suspects in the Hercule Poirot series. Poirot used the background information gathered on each character to structure his conversation with the person. Poirot was known for his penchant for solving cases through means other than traditional routes. For instance, he hired people to do the errands for him while he sat in a chair and used his little grey cells'; then he would talk to the people involved in the case.

In this chapter, we show the analysis of only seven books,[5] namely, *The Mysterious Affair at Styles, The Murder on the Links, The Murder of Roger Ackroyd, Murder on the Orient Express, Death on the Nile, Sad Cypress,* and *Five Little Pigs*. For the sake of simplification, we have left out the short-story collection. *Black Coffee* was novelized by Charles Osborne and hence has been dropped from this research. *The Clocks* and *Curtain: Poirot's Last Case* have been dropped on account of Poirot having no conversations with suspects in the text. The tables therefore depict the dramatis personae, their chief character traits, HP code, conversation style of Poirot, and dialogues to illustrate.

We now take each text and develop the interpretive patterns found in it.

The Mysterious Affair at Styles

Hercule Poirot was introduced in *The Mysterious Affair at Styles* by his friend Captain Arthur Hastings as "one of the most celebrated members of the Belgian police" and whose "flair had been extraordinary" as a detective.[6] He goes on to investigate the death of Mrs. Inglethorp, one of the benefactors of Belgian refugees. Table 3.3 depicts the interpretive patterns.

---

[5]Refer to the online additional material for the entire analysis.
[6]C. Keller. July 27, 2008. "The Mysterious Affair at Styles by Agatha Christie," [EBook #863]. The Project Gutenberg EBook of *The Mysterious Affair at Styles*, by Agatha Christie. https://www.gutenberg.org/files/863/863-h/863-h.htm (accessed November 2, 2018.)

Table 3.3 Characters in The Mysterious Affair at Styles[7]

Dramatis personae	HP code	Poirot's style	Dialogues to illustrate
Mary Cavendish			
Charming Loved her husband but could not show it proud wild creature	3.(i).G. Proud	Interrogative	"You are too amiable, madame. What I want to ask is this: the door leading into Mrs. Inglethorp's room from that of Mademoiselle Cynthia, it was bolted, you say?" [194] "Bolted?" [194] "I mean," explained Poirot, "you are sure it was bolted and not merely locked?" [194] "Still, as far as you are concerned, the door might equally well have been locked?" [194] "You yourself did not happen to notice, Madame, when you entered Mrs. Inglethorp's room, whether that door was bolted or not?" [194] "But you never did see it?" [194]
Evelyn Howard			
Efficient Smart and seemed to protect Warned Hastings of a possible murder Seemed aggrieved for the deceased	2.(ii).C.Efficient.b	Asked for help	"I want to be able to count upon your help." [107] "We are at one then," said Poirot, "for I, too, want to hang the criminal." [108] "But I must ask you to trust me. Now your help may be very valuable to me. I will tell you why. Because, in all this house of mourning, yours are the only eyes that have wept." [108]
Alfred Inglethorp			
Dependent on his wife for money Bad lot, obstinate Nervous	3.(ii).A.Bad-off.b	Warned	"I do not think, monsieur," said Poirot pointedly, "that you quite realize how terrible it may be—for you." [162] "I mean," said Poirot deliberately, "that you are suspected of poisoning your wife." [162] "I do not think"—Poirot watched him narrowly—"that you quite realize the unfavourable nature of your evidence at the inquest. Mr. Inglethorp, knowing what I have told you, do you still refuse to say where you were at six o' clock on Monday afternoon?" [163]

---

[7]Christie. 2001. The Mysterious Affair at Styles, Agatha Christie Signature Edition (London, UK: HarperCollins Publishers)

The Murder on the Links

Famous for the subplot where Captain Hastings finds his wife, Dulcie Duveen; the book deals with a murder mystery of a rich businessman who had asked Poirot to come anxiously—"For God's sake, come!"[8] The book had been said to be heavily influenced by French fiction of Christie's times and Sherlock Holmes. This book has been widely acclaimed to be unlike her usual kidney. Table 3.4 tabulates the interpretive patterns.

Table 3.4 The Murder on the Links[9]

Dramatis personae	HP code	Poirot's style	Dialogues to illustrate
Madame Renauld			
Middle-aged, magnetic personality Dignified Deeply upset over her husband's death	8.(iii).E. Resolute	Gently inquiring	"No," said Poirot gently, "it is a few minutes after five. Possibly the watch gains, is that so, Madame?" [63] "Madame, the front door was found ajar. It seems almost certain that the murderers entered that way, yet it has not been forced at all, Can you suggest any explanation?" [64]
Marthe Daubreuil			
Very beautiful Quiet Anxious	2.(i).D. Charming.b	Frightening (Threatening between the lines)	"Yes, mademoiselle," said Poirot gently. "It is quite true. But how did you learn it?" [92] "Suspicion is in the air at present, Mademoiselle." [92] "Will you ask me that question again, mademoiselle?" [208] "This. If you were to ask me that question again, I should give you a definite answer. Someone is suspected—but not a Chilean." [208] "Monsieur Jack Renauld." [208] "It was unwise to have tried to conceal the fact," ventured Poirot. [209] "The facts will tell against him," said Poirot. "You realize that?" [209]

[8]Christie. n.d. *Murder on the Links. Dr Mani.* http://www.drmani.com/murder-on-the-links-hercule-poirot/, (accessed November 22, 2018)
[9]Christie. 2001. *The Murder on the Links*, Agatha Christie Signature Edition (London, UK: HarperCollins Publishers)

Table 3.4 (Continued)

Dramatis personae	HP code	Poirot's style	Dialogues to illustrate
Leonie			
Housemaid Conservative Liked talking	2.(i).A. Bad-off.a	Sympathetic, Chatty	"What you say is very just, but what will you? The heart of a woman who loves will forgive many blows. Still undoubtedly there must have been many scenes of recrimination between them in the last few months?" [97–98] "Monsieur Renauld had not the temper of an angel?" [98] "Indeed," said Poirot. "And when did this quarrel take place?" [98] "And the dispute, what was it about?" [98]
Gabriel Stonor			
Athletic frame, well-built, good-looking Traveled across the world Assured	2.(ii).B. Imaginative	Interrogative	"Monsieur Stonor, the English chauffeur, Masters, had he been long with Monsieur Renauld?" [125] "Have you any idea whether he has ever been in South America?" [125] "In fact, you can answer for him as being above suspicion?" [126]
Jack Renauld			
Troubled relations with his father Haughty Boyish	2.(i).E. Nervous	Calm, providing a line of thought	"I will inform you, if you like, monsieur." [134] "Certainly I know. The subject of the quarrel was Mademoiselle Marthe Daubreuil." [134]

The Murder of Roger Ackroyd

Arguably, the most unprecedented twist in crime fiction is depicted in *The Murder of Roger Ackroyd*. Table 3.5 depicts the interpretive patterns.

Murder on the Orient Express

Murder on the Orient Express has been adapted into a television series and movies; one of the adaptations of the movie was recently released in 2017. Famous for the justice delivered by Poirot, this book is a marvel that takes

Table 3.5 *The Murder of Roger Ackroyd*[10]

Dramatis personae	HP code	Poirot's style	Dialogues to illustrate
Dr. Sheppard			
Country doctor Very respected and loved in the country Pleasant, helpful	2.(ii).H. Flattering	Friendly	"You must have indeed been sent from the good God to replace my friend Hastings," he said, with a twinkle. "I observe that you do not quit my side. How say you, Doctor Sheppard, shall we investigate that summer-house? It interests me." [130] "What do you make of it, eh, my friend?" he asked, eyeing me keenly. [131]
Geoffrey Raymond			
Pleasant, young fellow Ackroyd's secretary Youthful and efficient	2.(i).C. Efficient.b	Enquiring	"Mr. Raymond, this chair was pulled out—so—last night when Mr. Ackroyd was found killed. Someone moved it back again into place. Did you do so?" [120] "It is of no consequence," said the detective. "Of no consequence whatever. What I really want to ask you is this, Mr. Raymond: Did any stranger come to see Mr. Ackroyd during this past week?" [120]
Miss Russell			
Handsome, calm Rumored to having an affair with Mr. Ackroyd Very efficient	2.(i).J. Calm	Gave information and waited for her to break her composure	"Miss Russell—I have news to give you." [295] "I thought you might be interested, that is all," he said mildly. [296] "It is not quite all," he said smoothly. "This morning fresh developments have arisen. It seems now that Mr. Ackroyd was murdered, not at a quarter to ten, but before. Between ten minutes to nine, when Dr. Sheppard left, and a quarter to ten." [297]

---

[10]A. Christie. 2002. *The Murder of Roger Ackroyd,* Agatha Christie Signature Edition (London, UK: HarperCollins Publishers)

Table 3.5 (Continued)

Dramatis personae	HP code	Poirot's style	Dialogues to illustrate
Flora Ackroyd			
Very beautiful Though not everyone liked her, one couldn't help admiring her beauty Resolute	2.(i).D. Charming.a	Gentle yet crisp	"I see," said the little man. "But the police will do that, will they not?" [103] "All the truth?" [104] "Then I accept," said the little man quietly. "And I hope you will not regret those words. Now, tell me all the circumstances." [104] "See now, mademoiselle," he said very gently, "it is Papa Poirot who asks you this. The old Papa Poirot who has much knowledge and much experience. I would not seek to entrap you, mademoiselle. Will you not trust me—and tell me where Ralph Paton is hiding?" [186]
Hector Blunt			
Fond of hunting Talked very little Consumed, simple	2.(i).H. Consumed	Advising	"Ah! but you are to listen to me. I have more to say. The other day I speak of concealments. Very well, all along I have seen what you are concealing. Mademoiselle Flora, you love her with all your heart. From the first moment you saw her, is it not so? Oh! Let us not mind saying these things—why must one in England think it necessary to mention love as though it were some disgraceful secret? You love Mademoiselle Flora. You seek to conceal that fact from all the world. This is very good—that is as it should be. But take the advice of Hercule Poirot—do not conceal it from mademoiselle herself." [286]

the readers to the snowy winters of France. Table 3.6 summarizes the interpretive patterns.

Table 3.6 *Murder on the Orient Express*[11]

Dramatis personae	HP code	Poirot's style	Dialogues to illustrate
Mary Debenham			
Efficient Attractive Worked as a governess	2.(i).C.Efficient.b	Ego benefits in a conversational mode	"You are the only patient one; Mademoiselle," said Poirot to Miss Debenham. [42] "You are a strong character, Mademoiselle," said Poirot gently. "You are, I think, the strongest character amongst us." [42]
Princess Dragomiroff			
Extremely rich Aristocratic, paid heed to order and rules Ugly-looking	2.(ii).A.Well-off	Respectful	"Your full Christian names and address, Madame. Perhaps you would prefer to write them yourself?" [117] "Would you be so good as to give me a brief account of your movements last night from dinner onwards?" [117] "They are connected in this way, Madame, the man who was murdered was the man responsible for the kidnapping and murder of Mrs. Armstrong's child." [119]
Ratchett			
Too sure of himself Rich Ruthless	2.(i).G. Proud	Polite	"My *clientele*, Monsieur, is limited nowadays. I undertake very few cases." [29] "What is it you wish me to do for you, M.—er—Ratchett?" [30] "Monsieur, in my experience when a man is in a position to have, as you say, enemies, then it does not usually resolve itself into one enemy only." [30]

---

[11] A. Christie. 2013. *Murder on the Orient Express* (London, UK: HarperCollins Publishers)

Table 3.6 (Continued)

Dramatis personae	HP code	Poirot's style	Dialogues to illustrate
Caroline Hubbard			
Loved to talk about oneself Excited Found herself the most important	4.(a).(iii).B.Non-Imaginative	Gentle	"Tell it to me, Madame," he said. "But, first, pray be seated." [97] "You are sure of this, Madame?" [97] "You realized, Madame, that there was a man in your compartment." [98] "This button, Madame, may have dropped from the conductor's uniform, either when he searched your cabin, or when he was making the bed up last night." [101] "You have given us most interesting and valuable evidence," said Poirot soothingly. "Now, may I ask you a few questions?" [101]
Hector MacQueen			
Secretary to Ratchett Financially bad-off Efficient	2.(i).C. Efficient.b	Matter-of-fact	"Nothing. Let us advance with the matter in hand. I want you to tell me, Mr. MacQueen, all that you know about the dead man. You were not related to him?" [52] "For how long have you held that post?" [53] "What were you doing there?" [53] "Ratchett, as you suspected, was merely an alias. Ratchett was Casetti, the man who ran the celebrated kidnapping stunts—including the famous affair of little Daisy Armstrong." [84] "I should be more inclined to suspect you, Mr. MacQueen, if you displayed an inordinate sorrow at your employer's decease." [85]

(continued)

Table 3.6 (*Continued*)

Dramatis personae	HP code	Poirot's style	Dialogues to illustrate
Michel Pierre			
Nervous Respected, well-known antecedents Efficient	2.(i).E. Nervous	Gently inquiring	"And now," went on Poirot, "let us come to the events of last night. Mr. Ratchett retired to bed—when?" [78] "Now, Michel, I am going to ask you an important question. Where were you at a quarter-past one?" [79] "Good, my friend," said Poirot. "I wondered whether you would remember that. By the way, I was awakened by what sounded like something heavy falling against my door. Have you any idea what that could have been?" [81] "Do not distress yourself," said the latter kindly. "I cannot see that there has been any negligence on your part." [83]
Edward Masterman			
Trained butler Efficient Inexpressive face	2.(ii).C. Efficient.b	Interrogative	"Tell me in your own words exactly what happened." [90] "What were your duties exactly?" [91] "Do you know what drug he was in the habit of taking?" [91] "Did you know that your employer, M. Ratchett, was the principal instigator in that affair?" [93]
Greta Ohlsson			
Clumsy Susceptible to suggestions Amiable	2.(i).C. Clumsy.b	Interrogative	"I hear, Mademoiselle, that you were the last person to see the murdered man alive?" [108] "Did she ask you whether the communicating door between her compartment and that of M. Ratchett was bolted?" [108] "Why are you sure if you were asleep?" [109] "Have you a scarlet kimono, Mademoiselle?" [110]

Death on the Nile

Death on the Nile can be described as a tale of both love and hate. What happens when one loves way too much? Someone who has it all, does really have it all? Table 3.7 illustrates the interpretive patterns.

Table 3.7 Death on the Nile[12]

Dramatis personae	HP code	Poirot's style	Dialogues to illustrate
Mrs. Allerton			
Sincere, nice lady Did not like anyone else to get her son's attention Liked gossip	8.(iii).H. Flattering	Chatty	"You know her well, Madame?" [109] "You do not like her, Madame?" [109] "Yes, she is not happy, poor little one." [110] "Yes, he would not be ingenious." [111] "That would be like the Queen in your Alice in Wonderland, 'Off with her head.'" [111]
Cornelia Robson			
Clumsy looking girl Poor Pleasant and willing, amiable	2.(i).A. Bad-off.a	Friendly	"And you have enjoyed it—yes?" [132] "You have the happy nature, Mademoiselle." [132]
Miss Van Schuyler			
Rich, conservative Treated her poor relations like servants Looked down upon everyone else	2.(ii).G. Proud	Soothing	Poirot said soothingly: "Precisely, Mademoiselle. That is why we wish to free you from unpleasantness as quickly as possible. Now you went to bed last night—at what time?" [234]
Miss Bowers			
Efficient Brisk manner Cool and composed	2.(ii).C. Efficient.b	Interrogative	"Is Mademoiselle Van Schulyer's health very bad?" [205] "Will you tell me exactly what happened?" [206] "Now, Mademoiselle Bowers, I want you to answer this. Did Mademoiselle de Bellefort leave her cabin at all?" [206] "Does Miss Van Schuyler suffer at all from deafness?" [288] "Do you think she would have heard anything moving about in Mrs. Doyle's cabin, which is next door to her own?" [289]

(continued)

[12]A. Christie. 2001. *Death on the Nile. Agatha Christie Signature Edition* (London, UK: Harper Collins Publishers)

Table 3.7 (*Continued*)

Dramatis personae	HP code	Poirot's style	Dialogues to illustrate
Andrew Pennington			
Shrewd Ruthless, rich Something fishy about him	2.(ii).C. Efficient.a	Lied, chatty Accusing (later)	"I wondered if you had happened to come across some friends of mine who were aboard—the Rushington Smiths." [147] "His daughter comes into a considerable fortune, I understand . . . Ah, pardon—perhaps it is not delicate what I say there." [148] "I suppose, though, that the recent slump is bound to affect any stocks, however sound they may be?" [148] "One thought so at the time. Now—one wonders." [254] "I was wondering, Mr. Pennington, whether Linnet Ridgeway's sudden marriage caused any—consternation, in your office?" [355] "Something quite simple. Are Linnet Doyle's affairs in the perfect order they should be?" [355] "You were not so alarmed when the news of Linnet Ridgeway's marriage reached you that you rushed over to Europe by the first boat and staged an apparently fortuitous meeting in Egypt?" [356] "That on your luggage there are no labels of the Carmanic. The only recent labels of transatlantic sailing are the Normandie. The Normandie, I remember, sailed two days after the Carmanic." [356] "Monsieur Pennington, we do not believe a word of your story." [358]
Mrs. Otterbourne			
Gave herself a lot of importance Her style of dress made a ridiculous impression on people Self-conscious	7.(v).I. Engrossed	Conversational	"That is most kind of you, Madame. I will read it with pleasure." [66] "Oh, Madame, pray do not trouble yourself. Later"—[66] "Let me congratulate you, Madame, on a very lovely daughter," said Poirot, with a bow. [66]

Table 3.7 (*Continued*)

Dramatis personae	HP code	Poirot's style	Dialogues to illustrate
Rosalie Otterbourne			
Sulky, bad-tempered Good-looking, Resolute Dissatisfied with her life	2.(i).E. Resolute	Gentle, comforting	Poirot said slowly: "I saw, Mademoiselle, dark lines below a woman's eyes. I saw a hand that clutched a sun-shade so tight that the knuckles were white . . ." [59] "Why not say it—to me? I am one of those who hear many things. If, as you say, you boil inside—like the jam—eh bien, let the scum come to the surface, and then one can take it off with a spoon, so." [118] Poirot spoke slowly, choosing his words. "I could ask you certain questions, Mademoiselle, but I do not think for one moment that you would consent to answer them." [270] "You are accustomed, Mademoiselle, to carrying your own burdens . . . But you can do that too long. The strain becomes too great. For you, Mademoiselle, the strain is becoming too great." [270]
Jacqueline de Bellefort			
Very sad, bitter Had fought her way through life Vindictive, full of brains	2.(i).B. Imaginative	Advising, gentle	"Mademoiselle, I speak as a friend. Bury your dead!" [86] "Give up the past! Turn to the future! What is done is done. Bitterness will not undo it." [86] "I am not thinking of her at this moment! I am thinking of you. You have suffered—yes—but what you are doing now will only prolong the suffering." [87] "Go home, Mademoiselle. You are young; you have brains, the world is before you." [87] "It is deeper than that. Do not open your heart to evil." [91] "There, there. We know that you did not kill Madame Doyle. It is proved— yes, proved, *mon enfant*. It was not you." [208]

(continued)

Table 3.7 (Continued)

Dramatis personae	HP code	Poirot's style	Dialogues to illustrate
Simon Doyle			
Husband of a very rich woman Not coherent, took nothing seriously Boy-like awe, Financially not well-off	3.(ii). Bad-off.b	Matter-of-fact	"It would be pleasant if such were the case," said Poirot. [94] "I'm afraid not." [94] "Perhaps—revenge!" [95] "Well, you see, Monsieur Doyle, to begin with she is not a man." [97] "Ah, no, it was a quick romance—yours." [303]
James Lechdale Fanthorp			
Intelligent Watchful, lawyer Intense, not someone who travels for leisure Cool and competent in a state of emergency	3.(ii).I. Engrossed	Interrogative	"Aha!" said Poirot. "Now we begin to arrive. Let us, I pray you, be very precise. Describe to me exactly what happened." [200] "And it went under a settee, you say. Now be very careful. Mademoiselle de Bellefort did not recover that pistol before she left the saloon?" [201] "Then if there had been anybody at the port door looking through the glass you would not have seen him?" [202] "Did anyone hear the shot except the Nubian boy?" [202]
Mr. Ferguson			
Idealistic Fierce, tried to impose his ideas on others Knack for violence	2.(i).G. Proud	Matter-of-fact	"She is a type you dislike, eh?" [140] "Really?" [140] "Who told you she was one of the richest woman in England?" [140] "Me, I work with my brains and am not ashamed of it," said Poirot, answering the glance. [141] "My dear young man," said Poirot, "what a passion you have for violence!" [141] "I am not a middle man. I am a top man." [141]

Sad Cypress

Poirot plays the savior to the resolute girl who herself has given up on her chances to be saved. This is a great text on manipulations and projecting, as Poirot plays into the predator's hands while he plays them. Table 3.8 reflects the interpretive patterns.

Table 3.8 *Sad Cypress*[13]

Dramatis personae	HP code	Poirot's style	Dialogues to illustrate
Elinor Carlisle			
Looked aloof Sensitive, intelligent Proud, self-restrained	2.(i).G. Proud	Comforting	"I am Hercule Poirot. I have been sent to you by Dr. Peter Lord. He thinks that I can help you." [233] "You are very tired, are you not?" [234] "I have seen your—cousin, shall I call him for convenience?— Mr. Roderick Welman." [235] "You counted on your inheritance? That is understandable." [235] "Listen, Miss Carlisle. It is necessary that you tell me just what happened that day when Mary Gerrard died: where you went, what you did; more than that, I want to know even what you thought." [239] "No. For lies, tell a listener just as much as truth can. Sometimes they tell more. Come, now, commence. You met your housekeeper, the good Mrs. Bishop. She wanted to come and help you. You would not let her. Why?" [239]
Roddy Welman			
Fastidious but sensible Thought of money a lot; avoided unpleasant situations as and when possible Irritable, suspicious	2.(i).E. Nervous	Comforting, assuring	"I apologize—I apologize deeply! It is so hard—to be a detective and also a *pukka sahib*. As it is so well expressed in your language, there are things that one does not say. But, alas, a detective is forced to say them! He must ask questions: about people's private affairs, about their feelings!" [199] "Ah, but life is like that! It does not permit you to arrange and order it as you will.

(continued)

[13]A. Christie. 2001. *Sad Cypress*, Agatha Christie Signature Edition (London, UK: HarperCollins Publishers)

Table 3.8 (Continued)

Dramatis personae	HP code	Poirot's style	Dialogues to illustrate
			It will not permit you to escape emotion, to live by the intellect and by reason! You cannot say, 'I will feel so much and no more.' Life, Mr. Welman, whatever else it is, is not *reasonable!*" [201] "But surely, that was only natural! Your inheritance— that which was promised you—was in jeopardy! Surely it is natural that you should be unquiet about the matter! Money, it is very important!" [203]
Nurse O'Brien			
Cheerful, Full of vitality Capable Chatty	2.(ii).C. Efficient.b	Flattering, then formal	"It is a pleasure to meet someone so full of health and vitality. Your patients, I am sure, must all recover." [225] "Of course, in Mrs. Welman's case, it was a merciful release." [225] "You have no doubt at all that Elinor Carlisle killed Mary Gerrard?" [228] "If Elinor Carlisle killed Mrs. Welman, why did she do it?" [228] "If Mrs. Welman had lived to make a will, how do you think she'd have left her money?" [229] "You and Nurse Hopkins, you have agreed together, have you not, that there are some things which are best not brought out into the light of day." [230]
Nurse Hopkins			
Capable Homely, middle-aged woman Loved gossip, chatty	8.(i).C. Efficient.a	Clever, adroit manner Suggestive	"Miss Carlisle came down occasionally, I suppose, to see her aunt?" [168] "Ah," said Poirot, "I see you have made up your mind." [168] "You are quite sure that it was she who administered morphine to Mary Gerrard?" [168] "It is certainly difficult to see who else could have done it. Unless of course, she did it herself." [169] "One can never tell. The heart of a young girl, it is very sensitive, very tender." He paused. "It would have been possible, I suppose? She could have slipped something in her tea without you noticing her?" [169] "Yes. You weren't watching her all the time." [169]

Table 3.8 (*Continued*)

Dramatis personae	HP code	Poirot's style	Dialogues to illustrate
			"There is something else—a delicate matter. But I am sure I can rely on your discretion." [173] "I speak of Mr. Roderick Welman. He was, so I hear, attracted by Mary Gerrard." [173] "Although at the time he was engaged to Miss Carlisle?" [173]
Dr. Peter Lord			
Cheerful, spirited doctor Comforting Loved Elinor, scorned at her being arrested	2.(i).C. Efficient.b	Enquiring	"You and this young lady—you are affianced—yes? You are in love with each other?" [142] "What is the charge against her?" [142] "And the motive?" [143] "And in your opinion she didn't do it?" [143] "What is it exactly that you want me to do? To investigate this matter?" [143] "You wish me to look into the facts? To find out the truth? To discover what really happened?" [143] "But is it not a little unethical what you say there? To arrive at the truth, yes, that always interests me. But the truth is a two-edged weapon. Supposing that I find facts *against* the lady? Do you demand that I suppress them?" [144]
Mrs. Bishop			
Housekeeper Of conservative habits and views Disapproved of foreigners Aloof and implacable	2.(ii).G. Proud	Mentioned of his visit to royalty Chatty	"Marriage, alas, is fraught with dangers and pitfalls!" [179] "I expect," said Poirot, "that Mrs. Welman, before her death, must have been anxious to see her niece suitably settled in life?" [179] "The engagement was perhaps entered into partly from a wish to please her?" [179] "You surprise me. I had been given the impression that she was a very simple and unassuming girl." [180] "Nor I," said Poirot. "You interest me extremely, Mrs. Bishop. Some people have the knack of presenting a character clearly and vigorously in a few words. It is a great gift. I have at last a clear picture of Mary Gerrard." [182] "You mean, I take it, that Mrs. Welman might have

(continued)

Table 3.8 **(Continued)**

Dramatis personae	HP code	Poirot's style	Dialogues to illustrate
			left all her money to Mary Gerrard?" [183] Poirot mused: "The circumstances of her death seem quite inexplicable." [183] "I envy you, Mrs. Bishop. It is pleasant indeed to have nothing with which to reproach oneself after a death. Mr. Roderick Welman, I fancy, must blame himself for not going in to see his aunt that night, though naturally he could not know she was going to pass away so soon." 185]
Ted Bigland			
Was in love with Mary Gerrard Ready to talk Disapproved of anyone interfering in his matters Puzzled, child-like	2.(i).E. Nervous	Let the other man talk Regarded his opinions	"*But Mary Gerrard died* . . . and she did not die a natural death. Have you any idea—is there anything you can tell me to help me find out—who killed Mary Gerrard?" [188] "But, then . . .?" [189] "Yes?" [189] "An accident? But what kind of an accident?" [189] "Feeling is sometimes an important guide . . . You will pardon me, I hope, if I seem to tread on painful ground, but you cared very much for Mary Gerrard, did you not?" [190] "You wanted to marry her?" [190] "But she—was not willing?" [190] "You don't like Mr. Welman?" [191]

Five Little Pigs

In *Five Little Pigs*, Poirot reconstructs a crime that took place 16 years priorly. With only five people who could have committed the murder, the book functions on the differences cited between a murder done in a fit of rage and a cold-blooded planned murder. Table 3.9 classifies the interpretive patterns.

Data Analysis

We shall now consider the conversation style elicited as strategic responses with respect to the extracted HP code. The labeling here is based on the dominant characteristics of the character. One might note that the conversation

Table 3.9 Five Little Pigs[14]

Dramatis personae	HP code	Poirot's style	Dialogues to illustrate
Carla Lemarchant			
Attractive young woman Alive Attentive Intelligent, sensible	2.(i).B. Imaginative	Assuring	"You are making up your mind, are you not, whether I am a mere mountebank, or the man you need?" [10] "Rest assured," said Hercule Poirot. "I *am* the best!" [10] "Mademoiselle, I am honoured! I will justify your faith in me. I will investigate your case of murder. I will search back into the events of sixteen years ago and I will find out the truth." [18]
Philip Blake			
Prosperous Shrewd Jovial-looking man	2.(i).A. Well-off	Behaved in an outright foreign fashion, Lied about the writing commission Hardened, Interrogative (later)	"It is the public. They eat it up—yes, eat it up." [88] "It is human nature. You and I, Mr. Blake, who know the world, have no illusions about our fellow human beings. Not bad people, most of them, but certainly not to be idealized." [88] "You comprehend my position." [89] "Ah, but my dear sir, the why must never be obvious. That is the whole point!" [90] "And that, as you say, is where I come in! It is proposed to rewrite the stories of certain bygone crimes—from the psychological angle. Psychology in crime, it is my speciality. I have accepted the commission." [91] "It was an admirably clear narrative, but there were certain omissions, were there not?" [289] "Your narrative, shall we say, was not entirely frank." His tone hardened. "I have been informed, Mr. Blake, that on at least one night during the summer, Mrs. Crale was seen coming out of your room at a somewhat compromising hour." [289–290] "It is no matter who told me. That I *know*, that is the point." [290]

(continued)

---

[14]A. Christie. 2007. *Five Little Pigs,* Agatha Christie Signature Edition (London, UK: HarperCollins Publishers)

Table 3.9 **(Continued)**

Meredith Blake			
Middle-aged country gentleman Hesitant, could not be hurried Leisurely mental processes	2.(i).H. Consumed	Got references from Blake's friends Behaved foreign Interrogative (later)	"Alas—we do not live in a delicate age . . . You would be surprised, Mr. Blake, if you knew the unpleasant publications I had succeeded in—shall we say— softening. I am anxious to do all I can to save Miss Crale's feeling in the matter." [109] "As you will have seen in the letter I handed you from Miss Crale, she is very anxious to know everything possible about the sad events of the past." [109] "The truth," said Hercule Poirot, "can never be done justice to in a mere legal recital. It is the things that matter. The emotions, the feelings—the characters of the actors in the drama. The extenuating circumstances"— [110] "I want to know, Mr. Blake, the order in which your guests left the laboratory that day?" [292] "You are sure of that?" [292] "Let us go there now. We must be *quite* sure, you see." [292] "Reflect now, you are about to leave the room. You are going to the library where you are going to read the passage about the death of Socrates. Who leaves the room first—do you?" [293]
Elsa Greer			
Lively, youthful at the time of tragedy Strongheaded Very beautiful, described as Juliet	3.(ii).D. Charming.b	Comforting Interrogative (later)	"Because I realize this—this reconstruction of a past drama must be excessively painful to you!" [151] "You are sure, Madame, that to go over the past would not be painful to you?" [152] "After it was all over—the trial, I mean—did Meredith Blake ask you to marry him?" [294] "What did you say?" [294]

Table 3.9 (*Continued*)

Cecelia Williams			
Capable governess Used to being obeyed by all Lived in a meager income	2.(ii).C. Efficient.b	Told her the truth about Carla Matter-of-fact	"Very possibly. That you can tell me when you have seen her. You would like to see her?" [166] "Before we leave the subject of Carla . . .—little Carla Crale that was, there is something I would like to ask you. If anyone can explain it, I think you can." [167] "You mean that they were more like lovers than like husband and wife?" [169] "Did you ever say anything of that kind to Mrs. Crale?" [171]

Angela Warren			
Difficult, wild as a child Talented archaeologist now, celebrated lecturer Forceful woman, orderly mind	2.(ii).B. Imaginative	Straight, Matter-of-fact	"You have not kept in touch with her?" [186] Poirot said: "One might think so, certainly. A change of name—a change of scene. A new life. But it was not to be as easy as that." [186] "You approve, Miss Warren?" [187] "You surprise me very much indeed, mademoiselle. Everybody else I have spoken to—" [187] "I, at least, appreciated the difference. A sudden fit of ungovernable rage does not lead you to first abstract a poison and then use it deliberately on the following day." [188] "Yes—I think you are right . . . It is definitely a point of view, that. But all the same, Miss Warren, there must be more to it than that. What motive could Philip Blake possibly have had?" [198]

style varies with each code and sometimes even within the same code. Even if the style varies, it remains largely in an umbrella group. For instance, while the HP code 2.(ii).G.Proud is treated soothingly in *Death on the Nile*, it is assigned for a somewhat different reason in *Sad Cypress* when Poirot attempts to soothe Mrs. Bishop to get her to open up and divulge the truth. Hence, essentially the two styles fall under the category of "soothing."

The dominant characteristic of "Efficiency" can be applied to getting help or confiding, just as the characteristic of "Intelligence."

While dominant characteristics play a huge role in determining the conversation style, proclivity has an equally important role. For instance, consider the categories with "Bad-off" as the dominant characteristic. For the characters with positive proclivities, Poirot remains sympathetic in anticipation that his harsh ways might undermine their stature. On the other hand, when the proclivities are negative, he resorts to warning and keeping his conversation matter-of-fact. Table 3.10 establishes the strategic

Table 3.10 The conversation umbrella in an interpretive community

HP code	Conversation style	Book	Conversation umbrella
3.(i).G.Proud	Interrogative	*The Mysterious Affair at Styles*	Soothing Matter-of-fact
2.(i).G.Proud	Polite	*The Murder of Roger Ackroyd*	
2.(ii).G.Proud	Soothing	*Death on the Nile*	
2.(i).G.Proud	Matter-of-fact	*Death on the Nile*	
2.(i).G.Proud	Comforting	*Sad Cypress*	
2.(ii).G.Proud	Mentioned of his visit to royalty	*Sad Cypress*	
2.(ii).C.Efficient.b	Asked for help	*The Mysterious Affair at Styles*	Respect for efficiency
2.(ii).C.Efficient.b	Respectful, comforting	*The Mysterious Affair at Styles*	
2.(i).C.Efficient.b	Conversational	*The Murder of Roger Ackroyd*	
2.(i).C.Efficient.b	Matter-of-fact	*The Murder of Roger Ackroyd*	
2.(ii).C.Efficient.b	Interrogative	*The Murder of Roger Ackroyd*	
2.(ii).C.Efficient.b	Conversational	*The Murder of Roger Ackroyd*	
2.(ii).C.Efficient.b	Interrogative	*Death on the Nile*	
2.(ii).C.Efficient.b	Flattering, then formal	*Sad Cypress*	
2.(ii).C.Efficient.b	Told truth, matter-of-fact	*Five Little Pigs*	

Table 3.10 (*Continued*)

HP code	Conversation style	Book	Conversation umbrella
2.(i).A.Bad-off.a 2.(i).A.Bad-off.a 2.(i).A.Bad-off.a	Gentle and caring Sympathetic, chatty Friendly	*The Mysterious Affair at Styles* *The Murder on the Links* *Death on the Nile*	Gentle
3.(ii).A.Bad-off.b	Warned	*The Mysterious Affair at Styles*	Warnings
3.(ii).A.Bad-off.b	Matter-of-fact	*Death on the Nile*	
8.(iii).E.Resolute	Gently inquiring	*The Murder on the Links*	Gentle
2.(i).E.Resolute	Gentle, comforting	*Death on the Nile*	
2.(i).D.Charming.b	Frightening/ threatening	*The Murder on the Links*	Strict
3.(ii).D.Charming.b	Comforting, Interrogative (later)	*Five Little Pigs*	
2.(i).D.Charming.a	Gentle yet crisp	*The Murder of Roger Ackroyd*	Matter-of-fact
2.(ii).B.Imaginative	Interrogative	*The Murder on the Links*	Respectful
2.(i).B.Imaginative	Advising	*Death on the Nile*	
2.(i).B.Imaginative	Assuring	*Five Little Pigs*	
2.(i).E.Nervous	Calm, providing a line of thought	*The Murder on the Links*	Instilling confidence and providing a line of thought to the nervous personality types
2.(i).E.Nervous	Gently inquiring	*The Murder of Roger Ackroyd*	
2.(i).E.Nervous	Comforting, assuring	*Sad Cypress*	
2.(i).E.Nervous	Let the other man talk, regarded his opinions	*Sad Cypress*	
2.(ii).H.Flattering	Friendly	*The Murder of Roger Ackroyd*	Conversational and friendly
8.(iii).H.Flattering	Chatty	*Murder on Orient Express*	
2.(i).J.Calm	Gave information and waited for her to break composure	*The Murder of Roger Ackroyd*	Patience

(*continued*)

Table 3.10 (Continued)

HP code	Conversation style	Book	Conversation umbrella
2.(i).H.Consumed	Advising	*The Murder of Roger Ackroyd*	Foreign
2.(i).H.Consumed	Reference from friends, Foreign, interrogative (later)	*Five Little Pigs*	
2.(ii).A.Well-off	Respectful	*The Murder of Roger Ackroyd*	Respectful
2.(i).A.Well-off	Foreign, interrogative (later)	*Five Little Pigs*	
4.(a).(iii).B.Non-Imaginative	Gentle	*The Murder of Roger Ackroyd*	Gentle
2.(i).C.Clumsy.b	Interrogative	*The Murder of Roger Ackroyd*	Interrogative
2.(ii).C.Efficient.a	Lied, accusing (later)	*Death on the Nile* *Sad Cypress*	Clever
8.(i).C.Efficient.a	Clever, adroit manner; suggestive		
7.(v).I.Engrossed	Conversational	*Death on the Nile*	
3.(ii).I.Engrossed	Interrogative	*Death on the Nile*	

responses to the types of character profiles, thereby developing the coded norms of the interpretive community in which an interrogator functions.

Applied Lessons

An Interrogator in the Consumer World

The fictional basis used in formulating the HP code may seem restrictive and not all-encompassing of real-world situations. However, these labels apply not only to Hercule Poirot in their literal settings but also in analogous situations. These concepts can be used to formulate a code for deriving a personality code. The consumption pattern examples shall be instrumental in identifying the dominant personality traits. Interpreting the personality type and hence preempting how to make the individual respond develops a strong sense of responsive interrogation.

The interrogator asks himself: How would a certain personality respond to a question and thereby through the response open up and deliver information? Interrogation is always about eliciting information, whether personal, opinionated, prejudiced, biased, or objective. But through all these nuances of answers, the interrogator collates the dominant trends in tastes, preferences, and thereby choices—what is working in the market now and what is not, and with further analysis predicts what could work.

A market analysis attempts to decipher the narrative codes of a community—a community profiled with responders with dominant interpretive patterns. By analyzing Hercule Poirot in the Poirot series, we understand the responders through plot development. In the consumer community, we understand a consumer profile through their consumer choices. Martin Kornberger in *Brand Society: How Brands Transform Management and Lifestyle* defines a consumer as a *peculiar sum total of the products and services s/he consumes.*[15] Thus, these actions are narratives of choices, tastes, and preferences. These narratives on Twitter, Facebook, e-commerce logbooks, and blogs are traces of personality profiling. Table 3.11 presents consumer profiling scenarios that could be used to develop or predict consumer patterns as corollaries of the HP code. Here, we reflect upon **implied responders** and their profiling through their **consumer narratives**.

Consulting the Consumer Questionnaires

The HP code provides an investigative tool for information gathering and market research. Organizations such as *Nielsen*, *Kantar*, and *YouGov*, which provide market research for various parties, can use it to uncover relevant information. *Nielsen* studies consumers to give "the most complete view of trends and habits worldwide"[16]:

> We study consumers in more than 100 countries to give you the most complete view of trends and habits worldwide. And we're constantly evolving, not only in terms of where we measure, or who

---

[15]M. Kornberger. 2010. *Brand Society: How Brands Transform Management and Lifestyle* (Cambridge, UK: Cambridge UP)

[16]The Nielsen Company (US). n.d. *About Us.* https://www.nielsen.com/in/en/about-us .html, (accessed November 25, 2018)

Table 3.11 Analogues and identification patterns in consumer narratives

Dominant Characteristics	Analogues	Identification via Consumption Pattern
Proud	Snobbish, pompous, dignified, monumental	Likes oolong tea and if it is not available, would not have tea rather than settling for masala tea
Efficient	Well-organized, systematic, business-like, methodical	Knows which products to buy and the adequate amount, with little impulsive buying
Bad-off	Needy, underprivileged, insolvent, bankrupt	Goes for durable products rather than the fancy ones; for instance, choosing microfiber over cotton for upholstery even if they are priced the same
Resolute	Determined, purposeful, committed, single-minded	Likes a specific genre of movies, say, Shahrukh Khan's romantic comedies. Would not like him cast in roles such as Dr. Khan in *Dear Zindagi*; would watch *Dilwale Dulhania Le Jayenge* again
Charming	Delightful, endearing, good-looking, alluring	Tries a lot of things but there is a pattern in the chaos; one of the most difficult to spot, takes a longer time frame. Watches everything from *Silsila* to *Sacred Games*, but there will be only a specific genre that will have repeat value
Imaginative	Intelligent, sharp, canny, knowledgeable, perceptive	Knows when they want a black jacket with brown faux fur and will use filters on *Flipkart* to search for it; once found, would not take a lot of time in placing order with the best payment option available
Nervous	Hysterical, edgy, unsure, timid	Adds a lot to the cart and then gets unsure of the product at the billing; fiddles, and ends up buying none or only some of the items
Flattering	Praising, cajoling, honey-tongued, appreciative	Gives amazing reviews on *Zomato* but never visits the restaurant again
Calm	Composed, coolness, self-possession, poise	In the event of grievances, will comply with the rules of the institution without losing temper
Consumed	Absorbed, preoccupied, overwhelmed	Would not notice if their shampoo has oil retention or anti-dandruff qualities as long as it washes hair

Table 3.11 (*Continued*)

Dominant Characteristics	Analogues	Identification via Consumption Pattern
Well-off	Rich, wealthy, affluent, opulent	Will try products such as *Zampa Insignia* and *Fratelli Sette*, then decides which one to settle for
Non-Imaginative	Ignorant, dense, slow, suggestible	Follows the current trends; will buy animal prints and color blocks depending on the fashion, not thinking whether or not the fashion trend suits them
Clumsy	Experimental, awkward, ungraceful	Would buy anything they can most easily place their hands on; too shy to ask for the right fit. Would eat the white sauce pasta even if they actually like the red sauce
Engrossed	Preoccupied, engaged, absorbed, involved	Would go for products in lines of their profession; would keep buying books on archaeology if they are archaeologists

we measure, but in how our insights can help you drive profitable growth.[17]

Nielsen's emphasis on "constantly evolving" and in particular, through "insights" is the same impetus that helps, informs, motivates, and governs our very research endeavor. In effect, we are proposing how to "measure who and where" through our construction of the implied consumer.

In their own words, *Kantar* offers "the most complete view of consumers—the way they live, shop, vote, watch and tweet—in over a hundred countries worldwide."[18] On their web page, they publish the following illuminating narrative:

Our offer covers the breadth of techniques and technologies, from purchase and media data to predicting long term trends; from neuroscience to exit polls; from large scale quantitative studies to qualitative research, incorporating ethnography and semiotics.[19]

[17]Ibid.
[18]Kantar: Inspiration for an Extraordinary World. https://www.kantar.com/about, (accessed November 25, 2018)
[19]Ibid.

"Qualitative research," "breadth of techniques and technologies," "long term trends," "ethnography," and even "semiotics"—these are the key game changers for data processing in the contemporary scenario of informed decision making. The HP code simulates the narrative style of a character profile in a psychographic and economic setting with preferred tastes and preferences of the **implied consumer**—how we respond through narrative styles to which style of respondent. In other words, the *implied consumer* is a semiotic agent, and the Poirot study is a subliminal possible world study of semiotic agents and their narratives—"subliminal" because this is a possible world analysis. Poirot is a fictional response to real-time existence. The success of Poirot is a study in consumption itself because Poirot has been consumed over a large period of time by a legion of fans. Hence, Poirot itself is a semiotic response to a consumer market; it is symptomatic of the market needs—the consumer needs that are being fulfilled in the possible world of Poirot. Now what makes Poirot a rich study is his unique style of enquiry into a respondent's inner world. And in that fictional world is embedded Poirot's questionnaires with rich semiotic potentials; he taps into the respondent's inner world of fears, anxieties, anticipations, likes, and dislikes—in short, he helps to uncover the semiotic narratives of the respondent—the symbolic taste-maker and preference-consumer. In view of the foregoing, the HP code helps add to the real-time market world ways to measure the semiotic agent.

"What the World Thinks" is the motto of the market research forum *YouGov*, as it positions itself as "a global public opinion and data company" and intends to "explore the popularity and fame of anything and everything with YouGov Ratings."[20] Consider *YouGov*'s self-narrative on their web page:

> YouGov continuously collects opinions from around the world. Whether it's what people think about brands, politics, current affairs, or the things you talk about with your friends, we have data on it.[21]

---

[20]YouGov. n.d. *What the World Thinks*. https://yougov.co.uk, (accessed November 25, 2018)

[21]Ibid.

The variety of taste points identified by YouGov informs and is also indirectly informed of similar taste points in Poirot analysis—how you know a person—through her taste points, her choice of "brands," her opinion on "politics," her take on "current affairs," or what she likes to talk about "to her friends." Table 3.11 illustrates the process of constructing an *implied consumer-respondent.* For instance, you will know from her Internet buying over time if the consumer chooses shampoos that *basically* wash hair, even if differential labeling and positioning of the same products are *massively* announced—oil retention or anti-dandruff qualities of the shampoo fall on deaf ears. Tables 3.10 and 3.11 together demonstrate how you can identify these very functional buyers into the semiotic brackets of the implied consumers. The proclivity type is that of being very absorbed, consumed, and overworked, and various metaphorical correspondences may be developed. The conversations may be designed around first a suggestive mode and then venturing into an interrogative mode, and the HP code thus helps design the conversation stimuli for the semiotic type.

The present study requires asking questions to gain an understanding about the consumer and their preferences. The questions asked can be designed in a way that the respondent is comfortable. It is important to first understand the personality type and then administer appropriate questions for their type rather than going for a single stylization for all. In the days of Amazon venturing into "mass customization," the HP code is a small contribution to the same principle of developing mass customization, even in market research. The code helps ensure that maximum information is obtained about the *implied responder.*

CHAPTER 4

Ways of Informing

Amancha Vamshikrishna[1]

Review Speak

"LISTEN, and listen carefully," Vamshi said, sweaty and fearful, *"I don't have much time. This has to get to Captain America, do you hear me?! It's vital!"* He glanced around nervously, sensing imminent danger. Kim was still having trouble taking all this in. He had been minding his own business, browsing the leadership, psychology, communications section of the bookstore, when this young man approached him. On the surface it seemed a chance encounter, but as he spoke it became clear that he had deliberately singled out Kim as an accomplice. Vamshi held a small, somewhat tattered burgundy-colored journal, bound with a few thick rubber bands. *"I know it doesn't look much,"* Vamshi whispered. *"But it contains a powerful secret. A formula!"* He paused, noting Kim's look of doubt and apprehension. *"A formula for what?"* Kim stuttered, *"A weapon of some kind? A bomb?"* *"Nothing like that,"* Vamshi said, managing a small flicker of a smile. *"No, but it can be weaponized, and that's the concern."* Vamshi wiped his sweaty palms on his shirt, then drew his forearm across his forehead. *"Kim, I've developed a formula for unlocking the power of narrative."*

---

[1]Amancha Vamshikrishna, Societe Generale Global Solutions Centre, Bangalore.

As a writer himself and someone who'd had his own superhero encounters, Kim began to understand why he'd been chosen. He knew the power of story and of superheroes, and, apparently, so did Vamshi. "*Go on . . .,*" he said. "*It's called 'SAWI' and it has the power to propel the use of all forms of communication. To increase their potency very significantly.*" "*What exactly are we talking about here?*" Kim asked. "*Potentially anything,*" Vamshi continued hurriedly. "*Movies, internal business communications, diplomatic protocols and meetings, activist campaigns, and so on. Like I said, potentially any kind of communication that lends itself to narrative form.*" "*Well, that's fantastic!*" Kim smiled, eyes widened with excitement and curiosity. He already knew about the power of story to light up the whole brain, to increase oxytocin levels, and to encourage emotional connection and "neural coupling" between the teller and the listener. "*How does it do this, Vamshi?*" asked Kim. "*We don't have time for me to go into the details right now,*" Vamshi replied, again looking around anxiously, "*. . . but let me just say that I've managed to deconstruct narrative, by cross-matching the purpose of communication with particular narrative plots. My research has shown what plot types need to be used for different communication goals. When matched correctly, communication goes through the roof. When mismatched, it plummets.*" "*...and you're concerned this information is going to fall into the wrong hands?* asked Kim. "*Yes, Kim, exactly!*" replied Vamshi.

Vamshi breathed a small sigh of relief, knowing he'd picked the right person for the job. "*By itself, this formula is benign, but it can be put to all sorts of purposes.*" "*It could be used by those who would propagate messages of hate, fear and division. Those looking to control others?!*" said Kim. "*Precisely! Hydra's 'Counterfactual Intelligence Unit' has already discovered its existence and is using time and space portals to track me down. It's only a matter of time before they find me,*" said Vamshi and wiped his palms some more. "*So, you want me to take this to Captain America? Why him, and how?*" asked Kim. "*We can trust his integrity, his leadership, and his commitment above all else. Plus, he'll bring the full power of S.H.I.E.L.D to bear if necessary. Don't worry, he'll find you. Just keep this safe, I beg you!"* said Vamshi. As Vamshi turned to go, Kim raised his hand, motioning him to come back. *"Wait, Vamshi, how do you know this SAWI works?"* *"Well, you're using it now, aren't you? I mean you're matching Plot 7—'Plot creates a working example of information implementation'—with the purpose of this communication, to 'Sell an Idea!"* said Vamshi, beaming. *"That is what you're doing, isn't it Kim?"* asked Vamshi. *"Well, sure,"* the writer smiled. *"After all, you did say, 'This kind of goal,' selling an idea, 'is hugely targeted by academia whose purpose is to propose new ideas . . .' so I thought this would be most suitable,"* said Vamshi. Before Vamshi could finish his reply, they were interrupted by an old man who sought to squeeze past them in the aisle between the two shelves of books. *"Excuse me,"* said the man. *"I'm looking for the comic section."*

Vamshi and Kim looked at each other. *"Didn't he look like Stan Lee?"* Vamshi whispered. *"He sure did,"* Kim nodded. *"In fact, I think it was Stan Lee!"* Vamshi stood, staring blankly for a moment. For someone keen to enlist Captain America's help, he seemed disproportionately shocked to be literally rubbing shoulders with Stan Lee, creator of Marvel Comics. *"You best be going, hadn't you?"* Kim asked. *"Hydra may be here any minute, and I too need to get going if we're to protect SAWI."* The two men shook hands, exchanged glances, and quickly headed off, with a full movie and much adventure ahead of them. Vamshi sat back in his cinema chair, putting down his empty popcorn container, and turned to Kim and said, *"You know, I like that you've also used Plot 6, 'Plot conveys information as a surprise.' Even though that is best used for changing opinions, it still works."* Kim replied, *"Yes, I think the main thing is that as long as Plot 7 is there if your purpose is to sell this idea."*

—Kim Lisson[2]

---

[2]Kim Lisson, Principal, Karrak Consulting (*www.karrak.com.au*), Advocate for "artful leadership."

Abstract

In this age of information technology, nothing is as simple as conveying information. But what is difficult is how information is conveyed so that it is received in the way intended by the person who is delivering the information. In this chapter, a structure is proposed that helps identify ways to convey information depending on the type of information that is to be delivered. Structure developed is based on analysis of successful Hollywood and Indian Cinema. While Hollywood movies are analyzed to create a list of ways to communicate information and types of information, Indian movies are analyzed to develop a relation between both the movie industry and narrative domains. The resultant structure helps in designing information-conveying methods that are helpful for professionals involved in information-conveying roles—moviemakers, marketing teams, public relations teams, human resources teams, story writers, and so on.

Introduction

Conveying information has always been an art. It decides the fate of diplomatic relations between countries and also has an impact on brand value of multinational corporations. It is not just the information but also how it is conveyed that plays a major role in unfolding the consequences of information delivery. So it is necessary not only to choose the right information to deliver but also to choose the right mechanism to deliver it. Depending on the types of information, there are different ways to deliver information in an effective way. So to deliver information effectively, it is necessary to know different ways in which information can be delivered and also the most appropriate one for the situation at hand. So it is necessary to have a structure that helps us choose the narrative mode of delivery based on the type of information. Here, Hollywood and Indian movies are analyzed based on the information they are delivering and the way they choose to deliver, and a subsequent information delivery structure is developed. This structure can be used to find out an effective information delivery mechanism based on the type of information.

Data Rationale and Collection

Rationale for Data Collected

> "The pragmatic purpose of counterfactuals is not to create alter-
> nate possible worlds for their own sake, but to make a point about
> actual world."
>
> —Marie-Laure Ryan, *Possible Worlds, Artificial Intelligence,*
> *and Narrative Theory.*[3]

Whenever something is spoken that deviates from facts, a new world is created in which the spoken statement becomes a fact. The speaker is creating an imaginary world where anything that is not a fact in the actual world (AW) becomes a fact. It is like the speaker is narrating facts from another world. We imply from Ryan that the purpose of creating those alternate worlds is not to speak of something that has not happened in the AW but to speak something about the AW. Two examples in this regard will help clarify Ryan's theory.

1. Whenever an incident is spoken of and an alternate incident is imagined (what if something else might have happened?), the alternate world hypothesis is only to speak of the wishful consequences in the AW. The speaker has no interest in exploring this alternate world any further than analyzing its consequences in the AW.
2. Whenever stories are told with dragons, speaking animals, and so on, the speaker is creating an alternate world that is very drastically different from the AW. But in his or her creation, the ultimate motive is to convey information related to the AW. This information can be anything—human values, intellectual topics, traits of human personality, ethical and moral issues, and so on.

So though the worlds of mythologies, fantasy, and fictional stories deviate drastically from the AW, their use value is always to educate the audience on the AW. Throughout the ages, stories have been an effective way of conveying information. Stories have the ability of grabbing the attention of

---

[3]M. L. Ryan. 1991. *Possible Worlds, Artificial Intelligence, and Narrative Theory.* Bloomington, IN: Indiana UP. p. 48.

listeners, entertaining them with mind-blowing incidents, keeping them hooked to the narration, and then delivering the information effectively. *Jataka Tales* is one such example where moral and intellectual principles are taught to princes via stories on talking birds and animals. Analyzing these stories provides us with insights into types of information conveyed and kinds of narratives used to convey the message through a story.

In modern times, the most extensively used storytelling mechanism is the movie. So it is an obvious choice if we are to study the ways of conveying information through stories. There are different genres of movies that target different customer segments. Of all the customer segments, we are concentrating on the audience segment with maximum access to narratives through social media and alternate media forms—those of Generation Z who are flooded with information of different kinds. This segment of the population is under transition from fairy tale stories to real world stories—stories that convey harsh information such as, "all stories do not have happy endings." Even more particular is the identification of the transition phase in the lives of these Gen Zers—the adolescents. How do we narrate difficult information to these segments of individuals who are coming to terms with the AW? Movies do so. Movies built the alternate world (fairy tales). Movies also talk about coming to terms with AW. So if we can analyze movies that are targeted towards this segment, we can create a list of ways of information delivery.

Of all the genres, science fiction/superhero (SF/SH) movies are mostly targeted towards adolescent millennials—our target segment. And science fiction/superhero movies (SF/SH) are about problems and their solutions. Moreover, the millennial craze for the SF/SH genre is unquestioned. In order to have ample sample space of such movies, we collect a cluster of movies from the biggest science fiction movie production industry—Hollywood. Hollywood movies are chosen as first level of data to prepare the lists for types of information and ways of information delivery. For this data, top 10 successful SF/SH movies produced within 2012–2016 are collected.

Once the list is prepared, the types of information are tabulated from 10 successful Indian movies released from 2000 to 2016. To test the hypothesis, 10 unsuccessful Indian movies from the same time period also are collected.

Data Collection

To identify ways of information delivery, data on top 10 successful SF/SH movies within 2012–2016 is collected. Criteria for success are decided purely on the basis of revenue generated worldwide. Table 4.1 showcases the list of these movies.

Table 4.1 Science fiction/superhero (SF/SH) Hollywood successes within 2012–2016

Year	Movie	Revenue generated (million$)
2016	Deadpool	783.1
	Batman v Superman: Dawn of Justice	873.3
	Suicide Squad	745.6
	Doctor Strange	673.5
	X-Men: Apocalypse	543.9
2015	Avengers: Age of Ultron	1405.4
2014	Captain America: The Winter Soldier	714.3
	Transformers: Age of Extinction	1104.1
2013	Man of Steel	668.0
2012	Avengers	1518.4

Eight types of goals are generically met through stories or information delivery. They are as follows:

1. **Sell a product:** This goal is mainly achieved in marketing where the purpose of information delivery is to convince the audience to buy a product or service.
2. **Sell an idea:** This kind of goal is hugely targeted by academia whose purpose is to propose new ideas and develop new theories.
3. **Convey information:** People come across information with this goal in day-to-day life. Newspapers, traffic signals, weather reports, and so on fall under this category.
4. **Persuade to act:** Information with this goal is hugely informal. This approach is adopted by those people who do not have the formal authority to force the audience to act. Information under this category can include advertisements by celebrities conveying that "smoking causes cancer," and attempting to persuade the audience to avoid smoking.

5. **Change opinion:** Information that is normally delivered through debates has a goal to change the opinion of the opponents and the opponents' supporters. It can also include scientific data that questions superstitions or information that speaks about changing societal norms.

6. **Motivation:** Some information and stories have a goal of motivating the audience to do something difficult; something the audience can do but do not believe that they have the ability in themselves to carry the project to its successful completion. All the famous speeches by great leaders tried to achieve this goal.

7. **Develop, simulate, or generate interest:** Any kind of information that speaks about unknown or new things has a goal of creating interest in the minds of the audience. The speaker creates a desire to explore the topic further. The major motive is to create desire such that the audience works towards fulfilling the created desire *by themselves*. Information on new kinds of art forms, hobbies, career options, and so on tries to raise awareness and interest in the minds of the audience.

8. **Create followers:** Information with an aim of garnering followers or supporters, either for an individual or for a cause, can be placed under this category. Biographies of great personalities, great performances of artists, preaching by religious gurus, ideology of political parties, NGOs, and so on try to create more followers for an individual or an ideology.

See Table 4.2 for a tabulated form for the generic type of goals that any information providing/receiving practice contains.

Table 4.2 Types of information delivery goals (generic)

Goals of a Story
Sell a product
Sell an idea
Convey information
Persuade to act
Change opinion
Motivation
Develop, simulate, or generate interest
Create followers

Of the eight goals mentioned in Table 4.2, movies may not try to achieve the "sell a product" goal, unless they are themselves the product to be sold. So this goal is excluded and the final list for types of informing has only seven elements. For these seven elements, five Indian movies for each element are collected.[4] Table 4.3 is the list of movies arranged according to the type of information they convey.

Table 4.3 List of Indian (Hindi) movies and type of information delivery

Type of information	Movie name
Sell an idea	*Rockstar*
	Zindagi Na Milegi Dobara (translation: *We Won't Get This Life a Second Time*)
	Love Aaj Kal (translation: *Love Today and Yesterday*)
	Wake Up Sid
	Lage Raho Munna Bhai (translation: *Keep Going Munna Don*)
Convey information	*NH10*
	Bajirao Mastani
	Peepli Live
	Jodha Akbar
	M. S. Dhoni: The Untold Story
Persuade to act	*Udta Punjab*
	English Vinglish
	Rang De Basanti (translation: *color us spring*)
	Jai Ho (translation: *salutation of victory*)
	Aparichit (translation: *unrecognizable*)
Change opinion	*Pink*
	PK
	3 Idiots
	A Wednesday
	Taare Zameen Par (translation: *Stars on Earth*)
Motivation	*Dangal*
	Queen
	Bhaag Milkha Bhaag (translation: *Run Milkha Run*)
	Luck by Chance
	Rock On!!

(continued)

---

[4]Justification for categorization of movies based on the type of information conveyed is given in the later sections.

Table 4.3 (Continued)

Type of information	Movie name
Develop, simulate, or generate interest	*Talaash: The Answer Lies Within* (translation: *Search*)
	Rocket Singh: Salesman of the Year
	Chak de! India (translation: *Go for It, India*)
	Baahubali: The Beginning
	Wanted
Create followers	*Baby*
	Haider
	Kahaani
	Kaminey
	Ghajini

To test the hypothesis, a list of 10 unsuccessful Indian movies, as shown in Table 4.4, was also compiled. Failure of a movie is based on two criteria. They are as follows:

1. Ability to meet the expectations of prerelease hype at box office
2. Performance of movie compared to average performance of other movies of the lead actors

Data Analysis

Step 1: Identify the Plot Types in Hollywood Movies

With the data gathered on ten SF/SH movies from Table 4.1, we next turned our attention to the significance of plot in delivering the information, shown in Table 4.2. Based on the connection between Table 4.1 and Table 4.2, eight different types of plots were identified. Table 4.5 is the analysis of the 10 movies, with the plots identified.

Based on the analysis from Table 4.5, eight different plot styles are listed down in Table 4.6.

Step 2: Match the Plot Types to Successful Indian (Hindi) Movies

As the types of plot and types of information get listed out, the next step in this rather intricate psychographics is to create a mapping between information delivery and information types. This mapping tells what kind of

Table 4.4 10 Indian (Hindi) movies and their box office failure criteria

Movie	Reason to call it unsuccessful
Dil Dhadakne Do (translation: *Let the Heart Beat*)	Multistar cast. Grossed less than the average expected revenue of two of the big male leads and female leads. Also, considered one of the weakest films of the director; domestic revenues were barely able to meet the expenses of the movie.
Delhi-6	Despite having a star cast and a famous director, the movie is nowhere near to the previous hits of the lead artists.
Swades	One of the best movies of the male lead and the director, but the revenue was very poor even when compared with the average revenues of their previous movies.
Fan	When "100 million" has become a bare minimum standard for any big hero movie, this movie struggled to reach the mark.
Mohenjo Daro	This movie had huge expectations until the trailer was released. It was ridiculed on social media for incorrect historical portrayal, and that had impact on the revenues.
Roy	Known for his story selection, audience had huge expectations for this movie because of the male lead. They were only met with disappointment when they failed to notice any story in the movie.
Gabbar Is Back	Though it is a remake of various regional versions and has all the elements that are required to make the movie successful, its revenues were below average compared to other movies of the male lead.
Bombay Velvet	Released with much hype and controversy, this movie failed totally at the box office irrespective of having an excellent star cast.
Raavan	This movie simply failed to meet the prerelease hype it created with its trailers and teasers.
Ra.One	In spite of having one of the biggest heroes and heroines of Indian cinema in this science fiction/superhero movie as star cast, it was not even an average success in the career of these stars.

plot suits a particular type of information. To create this mapping, data on 35 successful Indian (Hindi) movies is collected; 5 each for an information type. Then for each of these 5 movies, plots are analyzed and the most recurring plot is selected as the best choice for that particular type of information. Repeating this exercise for rest 30 movies develops the necessary mapping.

Information Conveyed through Indian (Hindi) Movies

Table 4.7 expands on the information in Table 4.3 that showed the information type for the various movies; an Information delivered column has now been added to reflect the central theme.

Table 4.5 10 SF/SH movies and their identified plots

Movie	Line	Information	Plot number	Significance of plot	Information placement
Deadpool	Revenge of a lover	Superheroes can also be cool with vulgar language and adult content. At the end of the day they are humans and show human traits. Superpowers do not make you God. You are still human, susceptible to human tendencies.	1	Plot has nothing to do with message. Any story line, which conveys information, will do.	Information is displayed all through the movie.
Batman v Superman: Dawn of Justice	Fight between man and God	i. Man can fight God. ii. God (can be someone you look up to) too has emotions. iii. God, too, is critiqued.	1	No specific reason for how the last movie's reverence turned to hate in this movie. So this makes "plot" a necessary ingredient but not an important one. "Plot" is only to put man against God.	Create God and then create a need to fight God. "Need" is important. Need can be transformed to any other human created aspect—justice, upholding the law of universe, and so on. Information placement begins with the creation of "need" and it continues to be conveyed along with the story.
Suicide Squad	Powerful super-villains fight a witch	Power is power. It is neither good nor bad. The purpose to which the power is put to use matters	2	Create desperation to approach bad guys for help. End justifies the means. Significance of the "plot" ends with creation of desperation. "Plot" is only to create a situation. Otherwise, "plot" does not have anything new to offer in terms of story or narrative style.	Information is conveyed as soon as desperation is realized; at the same time the plot takes a backstep.

Avengers	Aliens invading earth. SH teaming up to fight them.	Team work brings out the best and worst in the person irrespective of having superpowers.	2	Plot is only to create a situation. Otherwise, plot does not have anything new to offer in terms of story or narrative style.	Create a situation that requires the information to materialize. In this case, create a situation where the group has to work as a team or it does not stand any chance of winning. Place the information in such a way that people have no choice but to accept it.
Doctor Strange	A neurosurgeon reads books on sorcery and becomes a sorcerer.	Knowledge is power	3	Every minute in the plot emphasizes "knowledge is power" without overdoing it.	Information is conveyed throughout the movie.
X-Men: Apocalypse	Men fight God.	Unity gives enough strength to defeat God. Even if you are God, you cannot win if you are alone. Even if you are God, you are bound to lose if your team turns against you in the last minute.	4	If part of the plot is against the message to be delivered, then that part should either be underplayed or turned to create a story to explain what happens if the message is not followed.	Information is conveyed a number of times at crucial intervals.
Avengers: Age of Ultron	A group of superheroes fight a human-made AI robot to save the earth.	Collateral damage is still damage. If you look objectively, humans are the biggest threat to earth.	5	Let the most hated character deliver the inconvenient information. One, information is delivered. Two, there is no backlash since people already hate him or her.	Information is not delivered directly, but it drives the story. Characters affected by information play major role in the story that keeps reminding the audience about the information.

(continued)

Table 4.5 (Continued)

Movie	Line	Information	Plot number	Significance of plot	Information placement
Captain America: The Winter Soldier	Save the world from HYDRA.	Distance changes people, but you should know why they change and stick to them.	6	Create a relationship between two people. Increase physical distance. Change them. Bring them close. Now see how things turn out. Distance matters. It would not be interesting if people change living under the same roof. Plot plays towards the information and reveals it as a surprise.	Information is placed as a surprise revelation.
Man of Steel	Fight aliens. Save earth.	Discover yourself. Your loyalty lies with the group you grow up with, not with the group you are born into. Does racial identity matter if you grow up with a different race?	7	Ask the question and let the plot work towards the answer. To speak about inconvenient things, sometimes all you need to do is ask the questions that lead to the information.	Create identity crisis and then let them discover themselves.
Transformers: Age of Extinction	Creators of transformers start hunting down transformers to destroy them.	You are safe only as long as you are useful to your creator. Or people are friendly only as long as they need you. Both these apply here since both creators and humans want to wipe out autobots.	8	Plot is to set stage for the action to take place. Unlike Avengers, this is not about just creating a situation in the beginning. Here, the plot is like a stage on which the story takes place, so the plot is there through all the acts. The plot is about the conflicts between transformers and their creators. It is only in this capacity that it is similar to Avengers. Interaction with humans is only to make the act easier to destroy transformers. Earth just provides an avenue for transformers to fight for their survival. Earth as a plot does not undergo any transformation throughout the movie.	Story is all about the characters' response to the information. So it can be said that the story is a consequence of information delivery. Here information is kept active in the minds of the audience through the characters that get impacted by the information.

Table 4.6 Plot types from SF/SH

Plot number	Plot type
1	Plot does not have any role in conveying a message.
2	Plot sets stage and then takes a backstep.
3	Plot reinforces information in every scene.
4	Plot tells what happens if the information is not followed.
5	Plot uses the antagonist to convey the information.
6	Plot conveys information as a surprise.
7	Plot creates a working example of information implementation.
8	Plot is absolute. Its characteristics do not change.

Table 4.7 Indian (Hindi) Movies and Types of Information

Type of information	Movie name	Information delivered
Sell an idea	Rockstar	Creativity comes out of pain.
	Zindagi Na Milegi Dobara (translation: *We Won't Get This Life a Second Time*)	You only have once chance to live your life.
	Love Aaj Kal (translation: *Love Today and Yesterday*)	People change, but not their motives.
	Wake Up Sid	Discover yourself.
	Lage Raho Munna Bhai (translation: *Keep Going Munna Don*)	Idea of Gandhigiri (translation: Gandhian practices).
Convey information	NH10	Life in the outskirts of Noida, a noted place in India.
	Bajirao Mastani	A true love story.
	Peepli Live	Exposing the current status of media.
	Jodha Akbar	Story of Jodha and Akbar.
	M. S. Dhoni: The Untold Story	Biography of a cricketer.
Persuade to act	Udta Punjab	Act against drug abuse.
	English Vinglish	Love yourself and do not be influenced by others' opinion of you.
	Rang De Basanti (translation: *Color Us Spring*)	Persuade to fight the corrupt system.
	Jai Ho (translation: *Salutation of Victory*)	Help others.
	Aparichit (translation: *Unrecognizable*)	Act against corruption.

(continued)

Table 4.7 (*Continued*)

Type of information	Movie name	Information delivered
Change opinion	Pink	Learn to accept refusal of a woman as a refusal.
	PK	Faith is good but not blind faith.
	3 Idiots	Study to excel, not for grades.
	A Wednesday	Hang terrorists; do not jail them.
	Taare Zameen Par (translation: *Stars on the Earth*)	Do not force children, understand them.
Motivation	Dangal	Women empowerment.
	Queen	Life does not end with a tragedy, it begins with it.
	Bhaag Milkha Bhaag (translation: *Run Milkha Run*)	Sports related motivation.
	Luck by Chance	Hard work coupled with utilizing opportunities.
	Rock On!!	Motivate youth to achieve something in life.
Develop, simulate, or generate interest	Talaash: The Answer Lies Within (translation: *Search*)	Generate interest in supernatural beings.
	Rocket Singh: Salesman of the Year	Search for opportunities.
	Chak de! India (translation: *Go for It, India*)	Create interest towards hockey.
	Baahubali: The Beginning	Create interest in VFX segment in moviemaking.
	Wanted	Create an interest in a new genre of movies.
Create followers	Baby	Creating followers for the lead role and the nation.
	Haider	Create followers for the male lead based on the type of character portrayed.
	Kahaani	Create followers for the female lead.
	Kaminey	Create followers for the male lead based on the type of character portrayed.
	Ghajini	Create followers for the male lead based on the type of character portrayed.

Plots used to Convey the Information

The next step is to analyze the plots of all these 35 movies and identify the most recurring plot under a particular information category. Table 4.8 provides analysis on plots of the movies for each category and the most recurring plot style for each category.

Table 4.8 Plots and information in successful Indian movies

Movie	Plot	Type of plot
	Information type	Sell an idea
Rockstar	Story of an aspiring singer who experiences pain and excels in singing	Plot creates a working example of information implementation.
Zindagi Na Milegi Dobara	Three friends go on a trip to experience life	
Love Aaj Kal	Two love stories set in different time periods to explain how people change with time but their motives do not	
Wake Up Sid	Story of a failed graduate student who discovers his passion for photography	
Lage Raho Munna Bhai	Story of a gangster who undergoes transformation after reading about Gandhi and starts preaching the latter's message	
Most Recurring Plot		7
	Information type	Convey information
NH 10	Movie conveys information about the outskirts of Noida all throughout	Plot reinforces information in every scene.
Bajirao Mastani	An informative movie about Bajirao and Mastani	
Peepli Live	Every scene in the movie emphasizes the status of media	
Jodha Akbar	A love story between Jodha and Akbar	
M S Dhoni: The Untold Story	Biography of Mahendra Singh Dhoni so much that some scenes are real-life footages	
Most recurring plot		3
	Information type	Persuade to act
Udta Punjab	Story of a rock star and a daily laborer stuck in drug mafia. Drug mafia is the absolute identity.	Plot is absolute; its characteristics do not change.
English Vinglish	Story of a woman who desires respect in the eyes of her family and achieves it.	

(continued)

Table 4.8 (*Continued*)

Movie	Plot	Type of plot
Rang De Basanti	Story of a group of youth who stand against the corrupt system. Corrupt system is the absolute entity.	Plot creates a working example of information implementation.
Jai Ho	Story of a person who intends to help others and gets stuck in power driven political system. Political system is the absolute entity.	Plot is absolute; its characteristics do not change.
Aparichit	Story of a person having multiple personality disorder trying to eliminate corruption. Corruption is the absolute entity.	
Most recurring plot		8
	Information type	Change opinion
Pink	When a male does not respect a "no" from a female (amorous gestures)	Plot tells what happens when information is not followed.
PK	An alien who has no idea of the concept of God. Stage is set when the "lead" comes across the concept of God, and the story unfolds.	Plot sets stage and then takes a backstep
3 Idiots	An example of what happens if your aim is to score marks rather than gain knowledge.	Plot tells what happens when information is not followed.
A Wednesday	Story of an unknown man who demands the release of terrorists to avoid multiple blasts in a city only to kill those terrorists himself.	Plot conveys information as a surprise.
Taare Zameen Par	Story of a kid who is considered poor at studies because of his lack of interest in studies only to realize that his poor performance was due to his mental illness—dyslexia.	
Most recurring plot		4, 6
	Information type	Change opinion
Dangal	Father dreams of daughters winning gold medal in wrestling and trains them to achieve it.	Plot reinforces information in every scene.
Queen	The bride's marriage is called off a day before. She goes on a Euro trip and discovers herself.	Plot creates working example of information implementation.
Bhaag Milkha Bhaag	True story of an Indian army man who wants to create a world record in athletics and about the hard work he puts in to achieve his goal.	Plot reinforces information in every scene.

Table 4.8 (Continued)

Movie	Plot	Type of plot
Luck by Chance	Story of an aspiring actor who is not only hard working but also smart enough to impress the movie world, its influential people, and gradually lands with lead roles.	
Rock On!!	Story of a group of friends who want it to make it big in the music industry.	Plot creates working example of information implementation.
Most recurring plot		7
	Information type	Change opinion
Talaash: The Answer Lies Within	Story of a police officer who tries to solve a murder mystery with the help of a prostitute only to realize that the prostitute is a ghost.	Plot conveys information as a surprise.
Rocket Singh: Salesman of the Year	Story of a salesman who identifies an opportunity and grabs it and starts his own business.	Plot creates working example of information implementation.
Chak de! India	Story of an Indian hockey player who decides to coach the women's team to win a world championship to prove his innocence. He overcomes the resistance of the team and gets them going.	Plot uses the antagonist to convey the information.
Baahubali: The Beginning	Story of a prince who tries to avenge the death of his father. Story is established in a fantasy world that takes VFX levels in India to an extremely high level and is visible in every scene.	Plot reinforces information in every scene.
Wanted	Story of an undercover cop who dons the role of a gangster with a mass appeal and I-do-not-care attitude.	
Most recurring plot		3
	Information type	Change opinion
Baby	Story of a secret service agent whose task is to track down terrorists and kill them. The movie is about heroism of character and any plot would do justice.	Plot does not have any role in conveying a message.
Haider	The movie creates followers for actors by offering them challenging roles.	
Kahaani	The movie is entirely driven by the performance of the lead role and it tries to create followers for the actress who played the lead role.	
Kaminey	The movie creates followers for actors by offering them challenging roles.	
Ghajini	The movie creates followers for actors by offering them challenging roles.	
Most recurring plot		1

Step 3: Match the Plot Types to Unsuccessful Indian movies

To test the hypothesis from Table 4.8, negative cases have been generated where the 10 unsuccessful Hindi movies that were selected and listed in Table 4.4 earlier, are tested against the Table 4.8 tabulations. Table 4.9 shows the unsuccessful Hindi movies, the information they convey, and the plot styles employed in each.

Table 4.9 Unsuccessful Hindi movies and their informative types

Movie	Information conveyed	Type of information
Dil Dhadakne Do	People are not their social status but their upbringing.	Sell an idea
Delhi-6	An NRI's perspective of India and how people change their behavior to impress NRIs and end up providing a different impression of the country.	Sell an idea
Swades	Persuade people to give back something to the society that nurtured their growth.	Persuade to act
Fan	Adulation is a self-reinforcing cycle.	Sell an idea
Mohenjo Daro	In plain words, it is the story of a revenge of a son.	Create followers
Roy	A film maker and a thief looking for closure in their lives.	Sell an idea
Gabbar is Back	Act against corruption.	Persuade to act
Bombay Velvet	Life is no fairy tale. From rags-to-riches story does not need to have a happy ending.	Change opinion
Raavan	Stockholm syndrome and only mythological characters are ideal in the mythological world.	Change of opinion/sell an idea
Ra.One	A typical good versus bad in a video-game format.	Sell an idea

Information Conveyed through Unsuccessful Indian (Hindi) Movies

Table 4.9 is the list of the unsuccessful movies (declared in Table 4.4) along with the information they deliver and the applicable category of information.

Unsuccessful Hindi Movies and their Plot Structures

Now let us review in Table 4.10 the set of unsuccessful movies from Tables 4.4 and 4.9, and define their plot structures that they have employed to tell their stories.

Table 4.10 Unsuccessful Hindi movies and their plot structures

Movie	Plot	Type of plot	Plot number
Dil Dhadakne Do	A group of families with internal conflicts go on a cruise. Plot unfolds on the cruise.	Plot sets stage and then takes a backstep	2
Delhi-6	Every scene revolves around the NRI providing him with an experience of Delhi life.	Plot reinforces information in every scene	3
Swades	NRI comes back to India and helps light up a village.	Plot creates a working example of information implementation	7
Fan	Uses the antagonist to convey the idea that fame is a two-way relationship.	Plot uses the antagonist to convey the information	4
Mohenjo Daro	Information conveyed as a surprise. Hero's past is revealed when he is exploring Mohenjo Daro.	Plot conveys information as a surprise	6
Roy	Two people looking for closure. Plot has nothing to do with how they achieve it.	Plot does not have any role in conveying a message	1
Gabbar is Back	Corruption as a concept is absolute and is dependent on the system in which it operates. Everyone thinks that they can contribute to reduce it, but it involves structural change in the system.	Plot is absolute. Its characteristics does not change	8
Bombay Velvet	A person goes from rags to riches, only to make the audience realize that happy endings are not guaranteed.	Plot creates a working example of information implementation	7
Raavan	Story is about transition of the person's feelings from hatred to respect. Every scene works on this transition.	Plot reinforces information in every scene	3
Ra.One	Plot sets the stage for good versus bad. Nothing much is offered in terms of plot after the characters are revealed.	Plot sets stage and then takes a backstep	2

Findings

Lucrative Ways of Informing—Structure

Based on the data analyzed, Table 4.11 maps the equation obtained between the type of information and the way of informing in narratives,

Table 4.11 Semantic algebra of ways of informing

Type of information	Way of informing	Plot number
Sell an idea	Plot creates a working example of information Implementation	7
Convey information	Plot reinforces information in every scene	3
Persuade to act	Plot is absolute. Its characteristics does not change	8
Change opinion	i. Plot conveys information as a surprise	4
	ii. Plot tells what happens if the information is not followed	6
Motivation	Plot creates a working example of information Implementation	7
Develop, simulate, or generate interest	Plot reinforces information in every scene	3
Create followers	Plot does not have any role in conveying message	1

as observed in successful movies. We call this the semantic algebra of ways of informing, an equation that can be evaluated for successful communication.

Testing the Semantic Algebra Hypothesis

In order to test the semantic algebra of ways of informing (SAWI) as derived in Table 4.11, a comparative analysis of the equation through unsuccessful movies is performed. Expected plot is compared with plot employed for a given type of information. Table 4.12 is a comparison of plot employed versus expected plot for the same cluster of 10 unsuccessful Indian movies.

From Table 4.12, it can be observed that the semantic algebra for conveying information holds in 9 of 10 tests. Therefore, from the findings, the following two statements are established:

1. The ways of informing play a major role in a successful delivery of information.
2. The effective way to inform depends on the type of information to be delivered.

Table 4.12 Hypothesis tested

Movie	Type of information	Expected plot	Plot employed	Match/ mismatch
Dil Dhadakne Do	Sell an idea	Plot creates a working example of information implementation	Plot sets stage and then takes a backstep	Mismatch
Delhi-6	Sell an idea	Plot creates a working example of information implementation	Plot reinforces information in every scene	Mismatch
Swades	Persuade to act	Plot is absolute. Its characteristics does not change	Plot creates a working example of information implementation	Mismatch
Fan	Sell an idea	Plot creates a working example of information implementation	Plot uses the antagonist to convey the information	Mismatch
Mohenjo Daro	Create followers	Plot does not have any role in conveying message	Plot conveys information as a surprise	Mismatch
Roy	Sell an idea	Plot creates a working example of information implementation	Plot does not have any role in conveying message	Mismatch
Gabbar is Back	Persuade to act	Plot is absolute. Its characteristics do not change	Plot is absolute. Its characteristics do not change	Match
Bombay Velvet	Change opinion	Plot conveys information as a surprise Plot tells what happens if the information is not followed	Plot creates a working example of information implementation	Mismatch
Raavan	Change of opinion/sell an idea	Plot conveys information as a surprise Plot tells what happens if the information is not followed Plot creates a working example of information implementation	Plot reinforces information in every scene	Mismatch
Ra.One	Sell an idea	Plot creates a working example of information implementation	Plot sets stage and then takes a backstep	Mismatch

Application

Using the Semantic Algebra Equation

In this modern age, when the attention span of human species is low, it is necessary to deliver information effectively in a short span. The effect the information has on the receiver determines his or her future actions. So, indirectly, the person who delivers the message can to some degree control the outcome of the receiver's actions by choosing an appropriate method to convey information. Various target segments can find the semantic algebra equation useful:

1. **Moviemakers:** As the structure is built on analyzing movies, moviemakers have the highest probability of success if they follow the structure. In India, particularly where the success rate of movies is less than 20 percent,[5] this equation will be helpful in creating a plot for a successful movie.

2. **Advertisement creators:** Advertisements have less than 60 seconds time to sell a product to a reluctant viewer. In this limited time, the commercial has to grab attention, create interest in the product, and then convey information in a way that convinces the viewer that the product is worth buying. Advertisement creators along with marketing teams can use the semantic algebra equation to develop effective advertisements and campaigns.

3. **Diplomats:** When it comes to relations between nations, it is more about how they treat each other rather than their intentions. So the ways of conveying information play a major role compared to the actual information delivered. This equation can be helpful in framing the message such that the information is delivered and also the unspoken intentions. Here is a recent example of that which occurred between India and Canada, which play by the equation.

---

[5]R. Cain. October 23, 2015. "India's Film Industry—A $10 Billion Business trapped in a $2 Billion Body." *Forbes*. https://www.forbes.com/sites/robcain/2015/10/23/indias-film-industry-a-10-billion-business-trapped-in-a-2-billion-body/#478bc56370d2, (accessed May 17, 2018).

Case 4.1

Bilateral Relations—India, Canada

Objective of the Discourse: The Indian government has to change the opinion of Canada on the pro-Khalistani movement. Consider the methods of bilateral relations as a plot of a story—dignitaries visiting each other's countries or meeting each other at a neutral location. The attitudes of the dignitaries might change and the outcome might change, based on how they treat each other. So for the type of information—change of opinion—there are two ways to convey the information:

1. Convey information as a surprise.
2. Tell or show what happens if the information is not followed.

   The first option cannot be employed since Canada is aware of the information that India wants to convey; so there is no surprise element. The other option is to show Canada what happens if it does not listen. Did India follow this path? Did it achieve what it wanted to achieve?

Analysis: Canadian prime minister visits India for a week-long trip. Here is a list of items that Mr. Modi, the Indian prime minister, generally, performs, when a foreign dignitary visits India:

1. Tweets, welcoming the dignitary
2. Breaks protocol, goes to airport to receive and hugs the dignitary, followed by photo ops
3. Takes dignitary on a visit to Gujarat (his home state)
4. Uttar Pradesh (UP) chief minister takes the dignitary on a visit to the Taj Mahal (internal political parties and their relations: UP and the current ruling party) (Taj Mahal is one of the great wonders of the world and is symbolic of love and friendship.).

Did Narendra Modi follow any of these processes? No, none whatsoever. He did not meet the Canadian prime minister until the sixth day of his seven-day trip. Let us consider the effects of the Indian prime minister's differential response on this account:

1. Everyone openly talks about the treatment that the Canadian prime minister received.
2. Justin Trudeau needs Sikh minority votes to win 2019 elections. Everyone knows it. But it is overlooked so far, since it is considered part of the electoral games. But this visit and Trudeau not reacting to the way he was treated showed the entire world his desperateness for this trip. Now online crowd cultures say he visited India for votes.
3. Nothing concrete resulted on the issues that both the countries wish to work together on.

Did India succeed in changing the opinion of Canada? This question is similar to asking a moviegoer if the movie changed his or her opinion. It depends on individuals. But is the information conveyed effectively? It is. People realized the motive of Justin Trudeau and his desperateness. It will have an impact on the 2019 Canada elections. This visit would be remembered by all the future dignitaries of Canada when they have to deal with India. If the Indian prime minister approached this visit in any other method, to convey his intentions, it would not have carried as much effect. For example:

1. If Narendra Modi had reiterated the Indian stand with Canada regarding the pro-Khalistani movement at every encounter, it would have made the world listening to this account "fed up" and eventually would have garnered a negative image for the Indian prime minister and sympathy for his Canadian counterpart.
2. On the other hand, if Narendra Modi had made India's stand clear in a single tweet and then stopped bringing up the topic, the world would have forgotten the tweet in a day or two.

Case 4.2

Human Resources Department

Organizations undergo constant changes to keep themselves aligned with the changes in their industry. One of the major changes an organization undergoes is trying to reinvent itself by changing its value proposition or the vision of the organization. This kind of change requires contribution from all employees. But what are the ways the organization chooses to convey this information about its changes? There are two types of audience for this information; the external world and the employees who are part of the organization. Based on the type of audience, the purpose of information varies.

1. For the external world, the information purpose is to **sell an idea**. Here, an attempt is made to sell the new principles the organization stands for. The organization is trying to say that it is evolving with time and hence proposing a new vision of itself.
2. For its employees, the information purpose is to **develop, stimulate, and generate interest**. To achieve its goal or reorient its vision, the organization needs the cooperation of the employees. They should be genuinely interested to make these changes a success because the effort requires a grass root level implementation. Hence, it is necessary to generate interest in the minds of the employees towards these new processes.

What strategies are the companies employing to achieve their purpose?

- For the external world, we generally notice organizations getting themselves involved in many PR activities or marketing strategies. But these strategies generally do not convey if an actual change is happening within the organization in line with its new vision. They try to reinforce the same information again and again without any concrete proof of changes happening within the company. Thus, the external world does not buy the organization's idea of change.
- The external world needs *a working example of change happening* in the organization, for example, a change in the top level executives and their policies or a change in the way the organization does business or with whom they do business. The world knows that you are changing only when you back it up with actions.
- For the employees, these *changes follow a top down approach*. Higher management makes a decision and expects the lower level employees to implement it. They can either treat it as **conveying information** message type or trying to **develop, simulate, and generate**

interest in their employees. Just passing down information and expecting a positive response will not help achieve the goal.

- These changes have to be inculcated as part of their daily routine. On a regular basis, employees should be made aware of the change initiatives and their contribution towards implementing these changes. Careful implementation is necessary to achieve these new goals. *Thus, the information must be reinforced on a daily basis until the goal is achieved.*

Further Study

The semantic algebra equation developed here addresses how to select an effective strategy to convey information. This structure can be further explored to convey information in terms of placement of information in a story or message. Two aspects of the strategy that can be expanded are as follows:

1. At what point of the story narration should the information be conveyed?
2. When is the emotional condition of the listener at a point at which the information can be effectively delivered?

Epilogue[6]

Vamshi's SAWI as a Subset of the Counterfactual Strategy in Conflict Management

Amancha Vamshikrishna has developed a nuanced model of the counterfactual strategy of persuasive communication. SAWI is an interesting model for governing conflict management in emerging economies in particular. In what capacity do we make this grand claim for SAWI?

- **Premise 1**: Vamshi followed the narratologist Ryan's footsteps when he concentrated on plot structures—in his case, he considered the most successful set of SF/SH movies produced in and by Hollywood.

---

[6]Pragyan Rath, Communications, Indian Institute of Management Calcutta (IIMC).

- **Premise 2**: SF/SH movies have a narrative plot that may be clustered in Ryan's third level of narrative genre, namely, the historical, legend, realistic plot structure. Unlike fairy tales, SF/SH "nudge" the audience to project their understanding of the counterfactuals through AW logic (here, scientific logic), and make adjustments with the "indeterminate" propositions (here, non-factuals). See Figure 4.1 to understand how Ryan's minimal departure operates in SF/SH movie plots. The imaginary (white circle) completely contains the factual (grey circle).

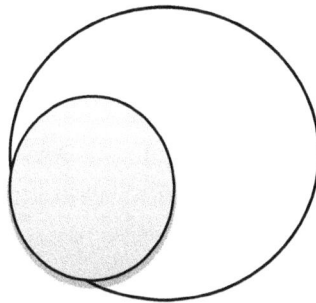

Figure 4.1 SF/SH plot and minimal departure

- **Premise 3**: As per our counterfactual strategy, the realistic plot is consumed by a particular kind of *crowd culture* with a particular kind of solution positioned in the counterfactual world, as illustrated in Table 4.13.

Table 4.13 SF/SH crowd culture and corresponding nature of strategy as per the counterfactual strategy[7]

Crowd culture	Order of System	Genre	Interpretive Process	Solution	Strategy
Marketing Culture (nostalgia automated)	Maleficent order	Mainstream Hollywood science fiction/ superhero movies	Minimal Departure	Minimal Pataphysics	Banal Strategy, Strategy of the neoreal

- **Premise 4**: As per Vamshi's own admission, the *crowd culture* consuming the SF/SH movies are Generation Z, or even the millennials and X generation who grew up with Marvel and DC—hence

---

[7]The Counterfactual Strategy from the Introduction chapter.

high on the nostalgia factor. In effect, there are consumers who were fed on Marvel and DC, even as intellectual capital, when they were kids.

But Vamshi then turns attention to an even more particular geographic clustering of this nostalgic-high consumer cluster.

- **Premise 5**: He tests his hypothesis extracted from Hollywood SF/SH genre on the biggest blockbusters but of the Indian (Hindi) movie industry. So the consumer cluster is now situated in the Indian emerging market, in the thriving movie production industry, popularly named after Hollywood—Bollywood. This emerging market population watching these big blockbusters need not necessarily be the same who are watching the Hollywood SF/SH movies. The author's lens of studying conflict management is through similarity of plot structures through movies across cultures. *Thus, crowd culture is not the predominant lens of study.*
- **Premise 6**: He "tests" the plot structures (and not the *crowd culture* types) derived from successful Hollywood SF/SH movie genres, and establishes that the successful Bollywood movies have had similar plot structures, and the unsuccessful ones generally have a mismatch between the information type and the way of informing followed by the successful formats.
- **Premise 7**: While Ryan studies the relatability between the counterfactual and the factual, Vamshi studies the information type and the way of informing, in the counterfactual itself. He concentrates on the format of the counterfactual, while Ryan studies the relation between the real and the fictional. As evident in Figure 4.1, as per Ryan's relational analysis, the concerned genre of counterfactuals contains the AW within it, while for Vamshi, SAWI becomes a format with a diverse range of plot types; he defines eight types—within the fictional horizon. The fictional horizon in Figure 4.1 is the white circle perimeter.
- **Premise 8**: Hence, all types of *crowd cultures* that have been immersed in these different narratives have been consuming the SAWI equation of problem-solving, in effect, in the counterfactual world.

- **Premise 9**: As per the minimal departure analytical model,[8] if the plot structures from SAWI are reproduced in actual activities for the corresponding *crowd culture* (all the types who are consuming these SAWI plot types), then the manner in which the problem was solved in the counterfactual can be replicated in the AW. Remember Figure 4.1 here: the actual is contained within the fictional horizon. Hence, that which works for the fictional would work for the real as well.

- **Premise 10**: This also goes to prove even if in a very imaginary environment, that most plot structures of the successful (so we may say mainstream) movies in an emerging market replicate that of the SF/SH Hollywood movies, even if the Hindi mainstream genres are not of the Hollywood SF/SH genre. It also shows the bandwagon potential in an emerging market such as India for SF/SH movies. Look at the revenue collection of current 2018 releases such as *Avengers: The Infinity War* and *Deadpool 2* (the latter even an adult-certified movie) in India, and that should validate the sway SF/SH movies have in the current milieu, globally and also in emerging markets, particularly, the Indian market. Table 4.14 lists the last five years SF/SH Hollywood top grossers in terms of their revenues in the US market, and the contribution to their global revenues through Indian viewership.

Table 4.14 Revenue generation of SF/SH movies in US versus Indian market[9]

Year	Movie	US Revenues	India Revenues
2013	*Iron Man 3*	$409.01M	$12,209,244
2014	*Guardians of the Galaxy*	$333.18M	$2,365,347
2015	*Star Wars: The Force Awakens*	$936.66M	$4,517,344
2016	*Rogue One: A Star Wars Story*	$532.18M	$1,143,293
2017	*Star Wars: The Last Jedi*	$620.18M	$2,462,280

[8]See Introduction chapter.

[9]Data collected from *IMDb* and *Box Office Mojo*. https://www.imdb.com/search/title?genres=sci_fi&sort=boxoffice_gross_us,desc; http://www.boxofficemojo.com (accessed May 25, 2018).

- **Premise 11**: One of two situations exists: (1) Contemporary *crowd culture* is majorly tuned into SF/SH movie plot structures, and if that is the major force of consumers, then as per the minimal departure analytical model, real-time communication should have the SAWI methods of problem-solutions; or (2) SF/SH Hollywood clouts through time have "nudged" an entire population of Gen Z, millennial, and X generations (in short, major labor force) beyond first world countries, from emerging markets; a scenario of cultural innovation running parallel with multinational firms and their sway on emerging markets that have open access to MNCs; hence, SF/SH movies are a good cultural innovator producing materials that need to be studied to understand their impact on "explaining" the AW, here the emerging market and thereby becoming models for solution provision for the AW in the emerging market.
- **Premise 12**: We must also remind the readers that the Indian Bollywood industry churns mainstream movies that may be more realistic renditions of SH movies in particular—Bollywood mainstream heroes are "heroes," and "heroes" are functionally meant to solve problems—factual problems and even unresolvable (counterfactual) problems.

Vamshi's Proposition and Its Legitimization

The use of fiction and its format converts a non-factual (*intent*) into the AW through a counterfactual semantic algebra—"selling style" or in Vamshi's words—"ways of informing." The "social bond" is then between the persuader, the *rule of* thought of counterfactuals produced by the community of fiction producers, and the consumers, who have been exposed to the counterfactuals (SF/SH) through their entire lives; these *crowd cultures* are "nudged" into getting into their virtual comfort zone, the underlying logic of comprehension, which is the *rule of thought* of the counterfactual operation.

Hypothesis: Through SAWI, Vamshi has developed a template for effective communication in situations of conflict. The identification of information styles has been derived from SF/SH movies. These styles have then been compared with movies that are produced in emerging markets. The author has concentrated on one of the largest Indian movie sectors—the Hindi film industry. Interestingly, the central protagonists in these plots have followed similar methods of information processing as those followed in the Hollywood SF/SH movies—the hero is the problem solver. In sum, the way the protagonist positions information in situations of conflict are useful insights for positioning of information in similar real-time situations because of the involvement of similar consumers. The emerging market moviegoers, in particular, are heavy consumers of both the Hollywood SF/SH movies as well as the Indian movies having similar plot structures. Hence, this consumer segment is already "unknowingly" accustomed to the communication styles in these identifiable plot structures with identifiable conflicts. Hence SAWI has a huge probability of being familiar, acceptable, and useful to the consumer segment hooked on the movies and, by extension, their communication styles.

As per the minimal departure analytical model, if the production of the nature of genre is realized, then using the counterfactual strategy equation, we can develop the attributes of the *subculture* where these "ways of informing" work well, because of mass consumption of the genre and its plot structures (the box office success of the movies prove the mass acceptance of the counterfactual strategy in *crowd cultures*). In the light of these premises, Figure 4.2 illustrates our contemporary nuanced problem-solving communication process.

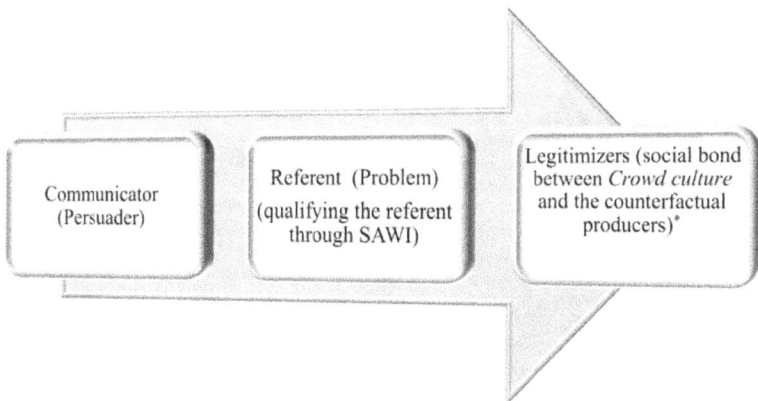

Figure 4.2 The SAWI counterfactual strategy of conflict management

Context in which SAWI works: The repeated revenue generation for narrative producers becomes the community's credibility building apparatus—the plot and its solution in the fictional format is then mass consumed; hence, the mass through the consumption becomes the legitimizing *crowd culture*.

CHAPTER 5

Ad Agencies: Producers of Disruptive Technologies

Anant Singh,[1] Karthi Prakash,[2] and Namit Jain[3]

Review Speak

Because of the way humans are hardwired, the role of ideas, story-telling, and interesting conversations in brand building will never get diluted. However, brand communication will continue to be shaped and influenced by new media and new contextual realities. It is common knowledge that advertising reflects what happens in society. Therefore, the trend (more a fad) of doing "higher order purpose" work that is disconnected from the product has to be seen in that light. Brand conversations are patterns that consumers buy into. What informs these conversations is a wider palette of considerations that go beyond product features and attributes. However, sustained brand building can never happen by staying away from or not referencing the product truth forever. It is not easy for serious advertising to be irrelevant. The role of the brand and hence its relevance and ability to move consideration scores are part of the research conducted by committed advertisers, all of whom track and measure ad effectiveness. So advertising could be

[1]Anant Singh, Associate Consultant, Alvarez & Marsal.
[2]Karthi Prakash Sa, Consultant, Deloitte Consulting.
[3]Namit Jain, Senior Associate Consultant, Bain & Company India Pvt. Ltd.

guilty of ineffectiveness, but irrelevance can only happen if people presiding over the assignment are less than ready for the task at hand. Books such as How Brands Grow have argued through empirical evidence that noticeability is more important and effective than differentiation. This may be in the fitness of things, given that the era of the unique selling point (USP) has been behind us for a while now. Differentiation must stem from a wide array of factors beyond product truths.

As the context gets more complicated, it also gives us many more dimensions to play with in the process of making brands noticeable and salient. This complexity offers a huge challenge for ad agencies to stay on top of the game and use creativity to circumvent reality. Finally, when we discuss what the agency of tomorrow needs to focus on, we must look at both the agency's as well as the client's (read: advertiser's) role in it because it is often forgotten that the client–agency relationship in the ad business is a symbiotic one. The marketing and hence the stated communication objectives are often too broad and fail to define the sharp role that communication can and must play. In the name of brand guidelines and discipline, we are guilty of setting so many "guardrails" that the communication fails to breathe and becomes uninteresting to the point of boredom or annoyance. Time pressures, cost restrictions, and an increasing apathy for nuanced and long-term thinking have become a part of our collective business reality. These factors force and shape advertising into possibly becoming more functional, left-brained and hence uninteresting. At times, it falls prey to the bandwagon effect of fads that are not necessarily useful. Finally, digital marketing and its seamless integration with consumer-led brand thinking is a territory that's far from settled. Essentially, the integration of minds that bring both brand-consumer-communication wisdom and digital marketing prowess is taking longer than expected due to a siloed existence. The journey to purposefully integrate digital marketing with consumer-led branding through mergers and reorganization of capabilities has begun in a big way. It is merely a matter of time before it all begins to work in a well-orchestrated manner. After all, it is the new reality and we need to make haste.

—Umesh Shrikhande[4]

Abstract

Advertisements sell products. They have been heralded as the twentieth century's greatest breakthrough in marketing. The popular notion celebrates advertising as the key tool required to capture the consumer's mind space. The advent of spot advertising (television commercials), which provides specialized content delivery in a brief amount of time, brought into prominence the advertising agencies. In contemporary times, spot advertisements have become all pervasive in their presence so that we have accepted them to be an integral part of what we consume. Such changes in social behavior are not without consequences. As Marshall McLuhan points out "it is only too typical that the 'content' of any medium blinds us to the character of the medium."[5] Delving deeper, we find significant departures in the consumer's attitude towards commercials over a period of time. This is partly due to the change brought about by the advertising agencies themselves. This chapter examines steps taken by agencies to be at the forefront of advertising by the introduction of subtle deviations. Whether these deviations are by chance or by choice is left to the interpretation of the reader. The analysis is primarily focused on television commercials of two mammoth agencies in the business of producing commercials—Lowe Lintas and Ogilvy & Mather. The insights developed are extended to the advertising industry as a whole through some examples of other agencies' actions, and industry progress is plotted to develop strategies for incumbents as well as new entrants.

---

[4]Umesh Shrikhande, CEO, Taproot Dentsu.
[5]M. McLuhan. 1964. *Understanding Media: The Extensions of Man* (New York, NY: McGraw, p. 9).

"It isn't the whiskey they choose, it's the image."

—David Ogilvy[6]

The Global and the Emerging Markets: India as a Case Study

Advertisements have been the mouthpiece for first-world countries, as the famous line from John Berger resounds from the cult piece—*Ways of Seeing*: "The great hoardings and the publicity neons of the cities of capitalism are the immediate visible sign of 'The Free World.'"[7] Advertisements or "publicity images"[8] as intellectually cataloged by Berger have been the persuasive tools for consumption. In effect, publicity images historically became "symptomatic" of flourishing consumerism, and flourishing consumerism historically became symbolic of economically advanced societies. Hence, the same symbols also play a major role in "positioning" the emerging markets as economic placements on a global map. But the disruptive displacement of consumer power has happened and is in rapid progression. According to a 2016 report from PricewaterhouseCoopers (PwC), there is a clear transition in the global positioning of BRIC nations and other "growth countries" (as termed by PwC in the report[9]) from "labor centres" to "consumption centres."[10] If advertisement images have been symbolic of consumption, then advertising and those who produce advertising have been important political as well as marketing forces for emerging markets to make their marks on a global business map.

Research Objective: Study Ad Agencies as Consulting Firms that Produce Publicity Images

Most researchers study advertising as a marketing feat, but very few highlight the consultants behind this marketing act—the advertising agencies. So we

---

[6]D. Ogilvy. 1983. *Ogilvy on Advertising* (New York, NY: Crown).

[7]J. Berger. 1972. *Ways of Seeing*. (New Delhi: Penguin, p. 131).

[8]Ibid.

[9]PwC. November, 2016. "Five Megatrends and their Implications for Global Defense & Security," *PwC, www.pwc.co.uk/megatrends*. https://www.pwc.com/gx/en/archive/archive-government-public-services/publications/five-megatrends.html, (accessed July 29, 2018).

[10]Ibid., p. 3.

attempt to study the producers of the publicity images, and not necessarily the images themselves. Second, we intend to study through the publicity images the communication strategies of the advertising consultants. We seek to not just understand how advertisement language has changed from the era of the labor-centric economy to the contemporary era of the consumer-centric economy, but observe how these commercial agents are architecting the future of publicity images when the very nature of publicity itself has transformed. The emerging markets are now realizing the interconnectivity of trade and investment flows between BRIC and growth countries (again validated by PwC),[11] which makes the traditional premise of publicity images as proposed in Berger (the symbol of the first world) redundant.

> **RH1** *(Research Hypothesis): So, when publicity itself is a redundant act of persuasion, what is the nature of persuasion in the world of advertisements in the contemporary politically liberating economic atmospheres of what PwC calls—the BRIC and Growth countries? Are advertisements dying, and if so, what do advertising agencies do in an era of "publicity/no-publicity"?*

Being part of the Indian scenario, we attempt to accomplish the following:

I.   Study the historical changes in the commercial functions of publicity images in India through the vantage point of the advertising agencies managing these publicity images.
II. Develop global lessons in the domain of advertisement consulting in probably a more endangered domain of business—advertisements.
III. Preserve the persuasive tool of business products and services themselves—advertisements, and
IV. Position the Indian market as a symptomatic study of the transitioning political positioning of a global consumer market that earlier was "viewed" as the labor market and is now enjoying being clearly considered by reputed consultant firms as one of "the macroeconomic and geostrategic forces that are shaping our world."[12]

---

[11]Ibid.
[12]Ibid.

And last but not the least,

I. Add for consideration a sixth megatrend that is a concern for global business, which is hugely missed by the major consulting firms when they make their typical lists of major global concerns, including the following:
    I.   Shift in economic power
    II. Demographic transition
    III. Smart cities
    IV. Technological shifts
    V.   Climate concerns

Thus, we add our sixth important megatrend for global businesses:

RH2: *6th Megatrend—macroeconomic and geostrategic force shaping global business—The transitioning position of advertising language.*

The reason for RH2 is evident. Publicity image reflects how a country conducts its business because the publicity image is reflective of one major business concern—how to communicate with consumers—how to be known—how to be visible. Hence, publicity image encompasses the concerns of all the megatrends listed by global consulting firms. And since the concern for these global firms is about the economic shift, then what better way than to help develop global lessons of "positioning publicity images" from the vantage point of emerging markets, since they are the most dynamic and disruptive of the global markets—they provide the fulcrum for global power shifts. Hence, it is more important to understand how businesses communicate in the era of economic power shifts from the point of view of an emerging market. The global lesson, then, is to envision the future of communication in a world of economic and political power shifts, and then appreciate the value of publicity images in a first-world country. The first-world economy is concerned with the already evident and impending expectations of disruptive power shifts produced by the economic game changers in politics and more significantly in consumption markets—the emerging markets. As consulting practitioners in global–local endeavors of business consultancy in India, we chose the Indian market to understand a parallel consulting firm—the sublimely hidden yet omnipresent firm—the advertising agency.

Data Collection

We analyzed more than 20 commercials, first from the two "symptomatically" influential commercial agencies that have been in the business of producing not just much-discussed commercials, but also generating templates of commercial-making techniques and strategies in India and the world over—Lowe Lintas and Ogilvy & Mather. We address their work as "symptomatic" because our study provides insight into the macro strategies of commercials that infiltrate consumer society. This society then feeds off their cognitive inquiries and desires from the most plausible, tangibly visible and accessible, and also the easiest and primary interface stationed between consumers and producers—the commercials. We then moved beyond Lintas and Ogilvy, as shown in Table 5.1, as we considered other agencies with strategies that reflect similar trends in visual communications.

Table 5.1 Advertisements analyzed and their respective ad agencies

S. no.	Advertising agency	Advertisement
1	Ogilvy and Mather	• Vodafone Zoozoos (Cellular services) • "*Mera Desh Badal Raha Hai*" (Government of India ad) • "*Chal Meri Luna*" (moped ad) • "*Govinda ek, handi anek*" (Fevicol)
2	Lowe Lintas	• "*Jaago Re*" (Tata Tea—Country awakening analogy) • "*Daag Acche hain*" (Surf excel—Puddle war ad) • "*Daag Acche hain*" (Surf excel—Dog ad) • Walk n Talk (Idea cellular)
3	Others agencies (Mudra Communications, McCann, Rediffusion, SapientNitro, etc.)	• "*Dudh si safedi Nirma se aayi*" (Nirma washing powder ad) (Purnima Advertising) • Dhara oil (Mudra Communications) • Airtel Musicals (Rediffusion YR) • Airtel Express Yourself (Rediffusion DY&R) • "Lead India" (*Times of India* ad) (JWT India) • Happydent White Campaign (McCann Erickson) • "*Why should boys have all the fun*" tag (Hero Honda Pleasure) (FCB Ulka) • "*Everest ka Tikha Lal*" (Indian spices ad) (Situations Advertising and Bhargav Krishnan of Eighty One) • "I love you Rasna" (Juice ad) (Mudra Communications) • Himalaya Neem Face Wash (Situations Advertising and Bhargav Krishnan of Eighty One) • Fuelled by Love (SapientNitro) • Scotch-Brite (Grey Group Bangalore)

Advertising Agencies: In Pursuit of the Underlying Context

Television commercials are a reflection of society's needs and depravity in a particular timeframe, and upon this need is built the brand positioning that provides pseudo satisfaction of the need. Let us take the illustration of British Airways advertisement titled *Fuelled by Love* (see screenshot of the commercial in Figure 5.1).

Figure 5.1 British airways: Fuelled by love[13]

This advertisement appeals to the egotism of the Indian populace wherein the reverse globalization happens—Indian culture is accepted and appreciated by the West. The advertisement tries to portray British Airways as the key connection that makes this global transfer possible, offering a pseudo sense of "Indianism" every time one flies on British Airways (the irony). The mastermind behind this irony was SapientNitro. In a similar manner we collated several such narratives spanning time, brands, and creative masterminds to try to understand the underlying context and grammar inherent in these commercial products, popularly

---

[13]Screenshot from "British Airways: Fuelled by Love," *British Airways*. February 1, 2016. https://www.youtube.com/watch?v=ZFb01yTR9bA&feature=youtu.be, (accessed June 25, 2018). Also see, S. Khan. February 5, 2016. "British Airways: 'Loving India Back Since 1924,'" *afaqs*. http://www.afaqs.com/news/story/47043_British-Airways-Loving-India-Back-Since-1924, (accessed June 25, 2018).

known as advertisements. The interesting observation in our trend analysis of the kinds of work produced by several such mastermind agencies is the rather "unsettling" discovery of "non-trends."

Hence, at the offset, we may as well begin with a premise that while one would observe broad strokes of emotional connect establishment with the consumer, there is no obvious common connection between the commercials made by these advertising majors. On a very basic level we realized that there is no one single formula for success. Thus, we wondered how to go about studying the works of these agencies and their contributions to strategic communication. So our next best premise was the following: *Lack of a single grand narrative is a formula for success itself.* In effect, underplaying the common connection is not something that arises naturally but is an artificially manufactured veil created by these agencies themselves. This conclusion stems from the fact that any product with common roots will have some shades of the root, unless there is a deliberate attempt by the makers to bury the roots. The following discussion examines some of the underlying reasons for the apparent lack of commonalities produced by these agencies.

Ad Agencies: Architecting Commercials as Brand "Differentiators"

An advertisement by definition needs to bring out a unique selling point for the brand. If any shade of linkage persists between two competing advertisements, the consumer will see one brand as an offshoot of another brand. This results in competing brands creating confusion among the public. Moreover, many services such as telephony are fundamentally the same. The service difference between Airtel and Vodafone is not a deal breaker while making decisions between the two. To differentiate such similar products, commercials are forced to sever any connections between them. Case in point: Vodafone ZooZoos (Ogilvy behind the cellular service in India) versus Airtel's musical (Rediffusion YR orchestrating India's premier music director A. R. Rahman—and his tone—for Airtel, another competing cellular service) as evident in screenshots illustrated in Figure 5.2.

Figure 5.2 (a) is a cartoon illustration (visual medium) while Figure 5.2 (b) is a musical (ocular medium). The presence of the ZooZoo (the visual cartoon in 5.2a) or the tone (musical note in 5.2b) supplies us with an

(A)   (B)

Figure 5.2 Comparison of ads from competing cellular companies:
(a) Vodafone: home delivery of new SIM[14] and (b) Airtel: The Airtel
music[15]

instant recognition of the brand pictured. Such brand distinction is hard to achieve in the presence of an underlying commonality.

Ad Agencies: Art Directors as Strategists in the Making

While the commercials are produced by the same umbrella company (Ogilvy or Lowe Lintas or any other), the production teams are made to operate in operational silos. Thus, the common connect between commercials are removed between the advertisement directors while it is brought into being—thus reducing overlap of ideas. While there can be a constant theme in the commercials made by a particular art director based on the individual's skills and background, advertising agencies as a whole seldom experience such commonalities. Table 5.2 categorizes the underlying techniques used in commercials by selected prominent commercial art directors.

Ad Agencies: Variations in Emotion Chord

One of the very successful campaigns by Surf excel—a well-known washing powder brand in India, in their *Dirt is Good* series of the campaign

---

[14]Screenshot from "Home delivery of new SIM. #HappyToHelp in-a-click," *Vodafone India.* March 27, 2018. https://www.youtube.com/watch?v=oMsQaGlZGAk, (accessed June 25, 2018).

[15]Screenshot from "A.R. Rahman old Airtel ad." *Donovan Francis.* March 2, 2017. https://www.youtube.com/watch?v=HLqnnMrAcow, (accessed June 25, 2018).

Table 5.2 Comparison of techniques used by prominent commercial art directors

Art director	Advertisement campaigns	Underlying technique
Piyush Pandey	• *Mera Desh Badal Raha Hai* (Translation: *My Country Is Changing*) (Government of India) • *Chal Meri Luna* (Translation: *Come my Luna*) (Luna Moped—automobile) • *Govinda Ek, Handi Anek* (Translation: *God Is One, the Vessels Are Many*) (Fevicol)	• Repetitive use of jingoistic phrases • Festive atmosphere of celebrations to the commercials
Prasoon Joshi	• Happydent White Campaign	• Use of visual imagery
Prahlad Kakkar	• *Everest Ka Tikha Lal* (Translation: *Everest's Spicy Red*) (Everest spices) • I love You Rasna (Rasna juice)	• Question and answer mode of delivery, children worldview
R. Balki	• *Walk the Talk* (Idea cellular) • *Daag Ache Hain* (Translation: *Dirt is Good*) (Surf excel)	• Common theme brought in forefront in initial seconds, then in repetition

led by Ogilvy—is the "Puddle war." The advertisement portrays a brother trying to console a sister by taking revenge on a puddle, the very puddle that dirtied his sister's clothes. The commercial resonates with every caretaker who tries to distract the child from her pain, by inflicting pain on a nonliving object. The advertising campaign was considered to be a smash hit, and the emotional connection with the brand reached great heights. On the other hand, in a very similar context, the "Surf excel—Dog" commercial failed miserably to connect with the viewers. It had a child play-acting as a dog to console the emotional distress of the dog owner while playing with dirt. Figure 5.3 illustrates these two commercials with their screenshots.

From the two examples illustrated in Figure 5.3, we might conclude that even similar campaigns fail to strike the same emotional chord twice. Hence, once-successfully portrayed emotional context cannot be reused by brands to develop new commercials. The repetition would be considered stale and would lead the viewer to compare to the older version rather than developing "connect" with the new one. Thus, a common connection, however successful, generally must be severed so that the commercial is seen as fresh and appealing.

(A)

(B)

Figure 5.3 (a) *Surf excel commercials: Puddle war*[16]; (b) *Surf excel commercials: dog*[17]

Ad Agencies: Delinking Advertisements from the Product

One of the more visible fads in the Indian advertising industry is the practice of delinking the commercial from the product, sometimes partially, but often completely. What do we mean by delinking the commercial? Delinking the commercial from the product simply means that the advertisement is no longer talking about the product, or in other words—*the product is not the main focus of the advertisement.* There is barely any talk about the product, its features, its functionality, or the need it aims to serve. The advertisement then simply becomes a grand narrative about "anything" but "something." Take for example the "*Jaago Re*" (translation: *Wake Up!*) campaign by Lowe Lintas for Tata Tea—a premium tea brand in India.

---

[16]Screenshot from "Surf Excel 'Puddlewar'—Daag Ache Hain," *Surf Excel.* July 26, 2012. https://www.youtube.com/watch?v=6o6JJIkamVY, (accessed June 25, 2018).
[17]Screenshot from "Surf Excel 'Dog,'" *footcandlesfeedback.* August 16, 2009. https://www.youtube.com/watch?v=tNE3l2LPiEY, (Accessed June 25, 2018).

The campaign was a series of advertisements promoting awakening of the masses, likening it to the process of preparing tea. In one particular advertisement of this campaign, a husband is shown lamenting about the dire state of the country, as he requests his wife to make tea for him. When asked to hurry, the wife replies with an answer how once the water gradually boils, it will gain energy, strength, and then ultimately, the water will change color. Eventually this process is used to create an analogy for the nation's "awakening" as well. One might argue that this approach is counterintuitive.

An advertisement by definition is trying to make the product more appealing to us, and thus needs to focus on the "appeal." A case in point is conceptual art arising from the movement of modern art. Conceptual art establishes the value of idea, concept, appeal, and even meaning over the object; thus, the creative consumer, the thinking consumer, and the more progressive consumer become the center of projection. So, what happens in modern or conceptual art?

The concept or idea (symbol) is now itself the meaning. It now represents itself.

In a similar manner, we may hypothesize the following for more insightful advertising:

RH3: *The advertisements have now come to represent themselves. They are themselves a commodity to be sold. They no longer derive their value from the product or the brand.*

After having established the prevalent delinking of the commercials from the products, it becomes necessary to analyze the rationale or agendas behind it. These agendas would then help us better understand the relationship between an advertisement and the product, and the product and the brand itself. Let's now examine three plausible explanations for this trend, analyzing each of the examples in the subsequent sections.

Data Analysis 1: Change in Consumer's Behavior

The standard learning hierarchy has always stated that the consumer collects all the information required to make a decision from all possible means, selects the product that matches his or her preferences, and then reaches a buying decision. This is also known as the high-involvement hierarchy where the consumer is heavily invested in every phase of the decision-making process:

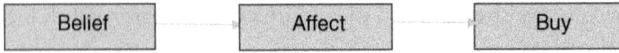

Belief	Affect	Buy

Based on this model, it made logical sense for the advertisements to be focused on adding value—providing more information of the product in order to affect the buying decision of the consumer. However, increasingly, brands have tried to convert the consumers' high-involvement purchase to a low-involvement decision:

Affect	Buy	Belief

As a result, advertisements these days are more focused on the "emotions." They intend to impact the consumer at the "affectual" level first, thereby inducing the purchase decision. For example, mobile phones are typically a high-involvement purchase, considering their price point and technicalities. However, by showcasing these mobiles as trendy and the "in thing," Apple's walled garden strategy has *arguably* accomplished the impossible—where Apple phones *alone* have software and facilities beyond mere communication attributes that *only* iPhone users can use, including music, camera and many other *lifestyle* activities.[18] Mobile phones have been made into a low-involvement entity, almost an instant buy product. Similarly, an advertisement for a scooter takes out all technical aspects, and solely focuses on an "in-group" identification, a feat led by FCB Ulka, as illustrated in the screenshot of one such "in-group" feature (here "young urban girls" in an emerging market like India trying to break the more rural patriarchal norms) in Figure 5.4.

---

[18]M. Murphy. August 3, 2017. "Apple's 'Walled Garden' Approach to Content has paid off massively," *Quartz.* https://qz.com/1045671/apples-walled-garden-approach-to-apps-and-music-has-paid-off-massively-aapl, (accessed July 27, 2018).

Figure 5.4 Hero Honda pleasure: Why should boys have all the fun[19]

Data Analysis 2: Universal Plot for Diverse Products for Similar Market

Advertising agencies are in the business of creating advertisements for their clients. The advertisements they create are their products. So, how do agencies sell their products to potential customers, while selling their current customers' products to their potential customers? Add to that challenge the need to appeal to a population that must choose among similar products. Following is an advertisement for the *Times of India* newspaper (TOI), as part of their *Lead India* campaign, designed by JWT India, as illustrated in Figure 5.5 screenshot.

The TOI advertisement attempts to convey the powerful message that the nation's strength is in its citizens and that the citizens can move the nation. The narrative does leave a powerful impression on the minds of the viewers. The imagery of a small school boy trying to move a huge tree is meaningful on a number of levels. What the child starts gets a nonchalant group of passersby "awakened" to community work, and they too join the kid in trying to move the tree that has stopped the traffic on a busy road. The smiling and cheerful faces of everyone greeting each other after having moved the tree are symbolic of Indianness.

---

[19]Screenshot from "1010_Hero Honda Pleasure why shold boys have all the fun commercials_TV ads," *Ads18.com*. February 6, 2015. https://www.youtube.com/watch?v=j6BNmbD0zOw&feature=youtu.be, (accessed June 25, 2018).

Figure 5.5 The Times of India: Lead India[20]

However, we see a problem (?) in the TOI advertisement. Let us re-place *Times of India'* at the end of the advertisement with *The Hindu*, the competing, and more intellectual, newspaper in India. Does the adver-tisement still make sense? Yes, it does. The child's act is still as touching and meaningful, the cheerful faces are still as symbolic, and the whole advertisement is still producing the same message as before—the nation's strength is in its citizens, and the citizens can move the nation if they wish to. This and many other such commercials bring us to our second plausible reason for delinking:

> **RH4**: *The agencies want to create commercials for their current clients such that their potential clients see their brands in those commercials.*

Let us better understand how the sentiment documented in RH4 works. Suppose that Ogilvy & Mather creates the ZooZoo campaign for Vodafone. Now it is in its own interest that the advertisements are general enough for them to be relatable to other brands such as Idea, Airtel, and

---

[20]Screenshot from "Lead India—The Tree," *milinddequinox*. February 25, 2010. youtu .be/GPeeZ6viNgY, (accessed June 25, 2018).

countless others searching for "mileage." So the question now is whether the Airtel makers see their brand in my advertisement for Vodafone. Is it possible for me to make the marketing head of Airtel look at the Vodafone advertisement and immediately say, "Gosh! I would like these guys to make commercials for me too!"

What happens, on the other hand, if the commercials are very brand-specific? The Airtel head would probably then say, "Well, these guys make good commercials, but will they be able to make equally good ones for my brand too? Can't be so sure." That is why making general advertisements is important for Ogilvy. It allows them to pitch to the other brands later on. Moreover, the current client is also happy to see its commercial becoming so famous and is inclined to believe that its brand's popularity is consistent with its advertisement campaign's popularity. What then is the incentive for the advertising agency to make product-focused commercials? Nothing!

Attributes Arrived at from the Advertisement Data Analyses

Having contended with the notion that advertising agencies intentionally delink the product from the commercial to satisfy their commercial interests, it would be worthwhile to consider that the agencies are not really concerned about the product they are advertising.

Instead:

> **RH5**: *Through advertising, they want to advertise the medium of advertising.*

Let us consider the first attribute that we derive from RH5.

Attribute 1: Existential Paradox

In today's business climate, one could opine that everything is about selling yourself. Individuals sell themselves (and their ideas!) at their workplace; companies sell their products to the market; even religions try to sell themselves.

How then, do advertising agencies, responsible for selling others' products, sell themselves?

The biggest constraint that these agencies face is that they cannot bring themselves to the forefront. Why? Commercials and brands share the consumer's mind space. As a consumer, you have a limited attention span, limited memory, and limited effectual space. This space is contested for competing brands and their advertisement as well. This dilemma is analogous to a film and its director. It often happens that the director becomes more popular than the movie or the message that the movie is trying to communicate. However, brands cannot afford to let that happen, for obvious reasons. Hence, advertising agencies are compelled to maintain a low profile and keep themselves in the background. One rarely gets to know the creator of any advertisement.

So, how do advertisement agencies stay relevant as individual entities and as an industry altogether?

Since motion advertisements compete with other promotion media including print commercials, in-store promotion, radio ads, personal selling, and many more, they are in the constant challenge of portraying themselves as the most effective way to reach customers and "affect" them. Proving this might not be possible through simple, direct advertisements that focus on the products. Hence, the agencies try to stay relevant by projecting the preferred medium of promotion by advertising the medium through the apparent "product" advertisements. Consider the example illustrated in the screenshots in Figure 5.6. In the advertisement,

Figure 5.6 Screenshots from Emami Fair and Handsome[21]

---

[21]Screenshot from "Emami Fair and Handsome—Shahrukh Khan," *afaqs!* July 5, 2013. https://www.youtube.com/watch?v=uGr2QwDv_P8&feature=youtu.be, (accessed June 25, 2018).

there is a direct callout to the attributes of the beauty product; however it has little impact when compared to the short video of a successful celebrity attributing their success to the product. A short 30-second video of the "from-rags-to-riches" story leaves a greater impact than an outright callout to the product, thus showcasing how the medium that enables the story leaves a greater impact rather than the product details itself.

Thus, an advertisement created by an advertising agency seeks to send out a message about the positioning of the product. At the same time, it seeks to sell itself. However, as pointed out earlier, it needs to do that almost conspicuously, keeping the brands' interest at the forefront. This brings us to our main argument in this chapter:

> **RH6**: *Advertisers advertise the medium of advertising, and not the product, through all their advertisements.*

Attribute 2: Prolonged Use of Anonymity

While print advertisements need to catch eyes, television commercials just need to please the audience. They do not have to make efforts to catch our attention. We are more likely to sit through the commercial during the break of a cricket match, but a poster in the morning newspaper will have to be really striking and attractive to catch your attention in the first place. How then, is this advantage exploited? We see innumerable commercials wherein the product is introduced at a very late stage in the advertisement. For example, in Figure 5.7, the product is brought forth only in the 70th second of a 75-second video. Till the product is called out in the last five seconds, there is not a single reference to the product category or the product. The onus is on the viewer to establish "the connect" between the product and the narrative, thus actively engaging the viewer till the last second. The commercial is part of the Airtel "Express Yourself" campaign by Rediffusion DY&R.

Attribute 3: Use of Relatable Characters

The ability to establish a context, work around a story, use emotions, and work in a desired setting allow television commercials to create

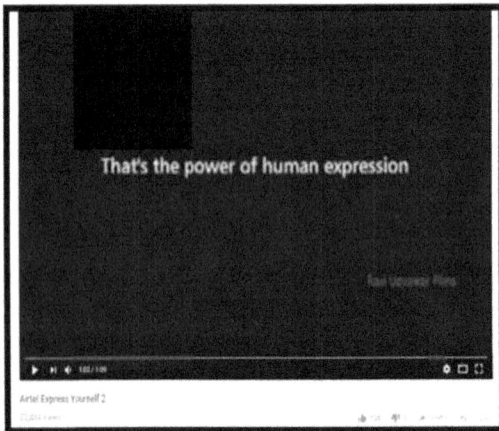

Figure 5.7 Airtel's Express Yourself advertisement[22]

characters that are much more relatable for us. Consider an Indian woman's photo on a print poster by Scotch-Brite, in which she is trying to convince you how easy her life has become since she started using

[22]Screenshot from "Airtel Express Yourself 2" *RaviUdyawarfilms*. March 30, 2010. https://www.youtube.com/watch?v=C3ZHg3tnXZI, (accessed June 25, 2018).

the vessel scrubber. On the other hand, Grey Group Bangalore depicts a typical Indian housewife-looking woman, rubbing and scratching her utensils really hard, sweating like anything, and showing all her frustration from the excessive effort she has to put in daily. Which one of these two would you see yourself more in? Whose situation would be more relatable? Whose emotion would be felt more? Witness the comparative narrative in Figure 5.8.

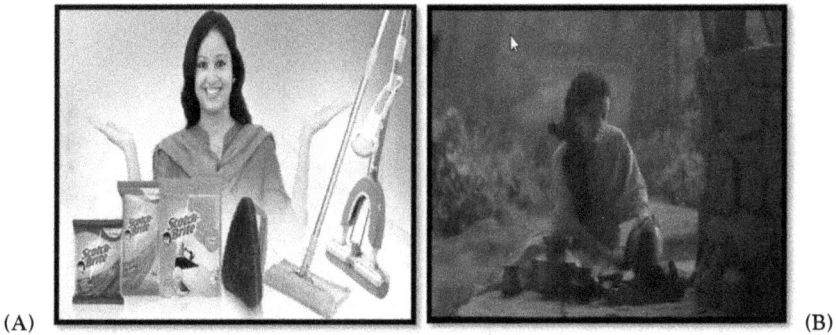

(A)   (B)

Figure 5.8 Comparison of *Scotch-Brite advertisements*

(a) Scotch-Brite: Print Ad[23] (b) Scotch-Brite by Grey Agency[24]

Attribute 4: Grey Emphasis

By grey emphasis, we are referring to an advertisement's ability to use subtlety and moderation in depicting contrasts. A television advertisement can make do by showing subtle contrast or "grey emphasis" as we call it, while other posters tend to use starker and often disturbing contrasts. Why? The reasoning goes back to our earlier point on grabbing eyes versus pleasing the audience. As a result, a hair transplant generally looks as unattractive and black-white as illustrated in Figure 5.9 in a print poster.

Even most pimple-removal face wash commercials on television would be nowhere close to being so hard to consume as in a print ad, as illustrated in Figure 5.10.

---

[23]Taken from a personal collection from a newspaper.
[24]Screenshot from "Scotch-Brite® Scrub Pad with Stain Cutters which helps it lasts longer*," *ScotchBriteIndia*. June 25, 2015. https://www.youtube.com/watch?v=LL50Q0EEE1k, (accessed June 25, 2018).

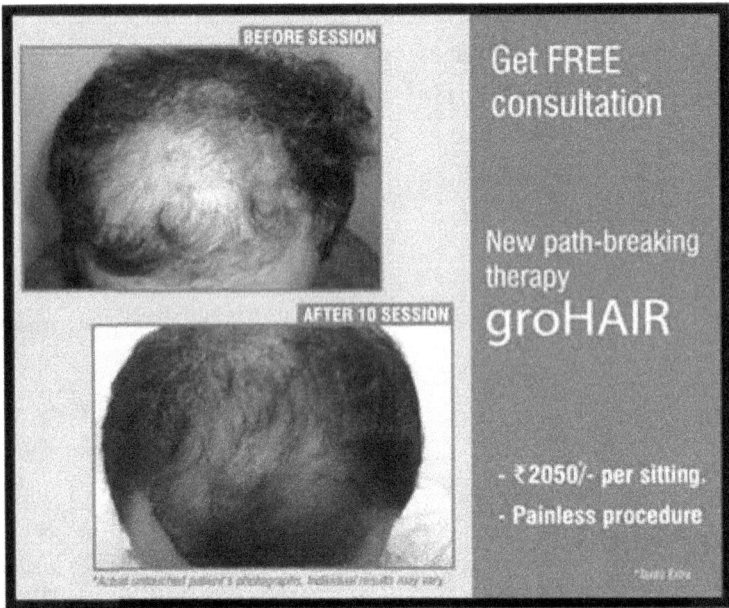

Figure 5.9 Print poster of a hair transplant client in an ad published in a leading daily of North India[25]

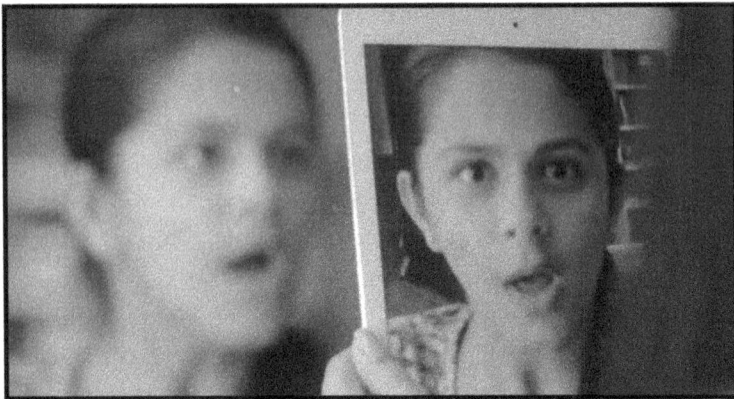

Figure 5.10 Himalaya Neem Face Wash: Sisters[26]

---

[25]From personal collection of newspaper cuttings.

[26]Screenshot from "Himalaya Neem Face Wash: Sisters," *Code Red Films.* June 3, 2015. https://www.youtube.com/watch?v=pd_TCox_r4w&feature=youtu.be, (accessed June 25, 2018).

Attribute 5: Multishot Attacks

This is probably the most common and most obvious of the motifs. A television advertisement has the distinct privilege of getting access to the same set of audience repeatedly. This allows the advertisers to affect the audience in multiple small attacks—in "campaigns" rather than single prints. That explains the prevalence of a series of advertisements being released one after another, sometimes with a story binding them together, and on other occasions, just a common theme. Consider Figure 5.11 with the ZooZoo multishots.

Figure 5.11 Vodafone ZooZoo[27]

The best example of the multishot motif would be the phenomenally popular ZooZoo campaign by Vodafone orchestrated by Ogilvy. Since 2009, the ZooZoo has accurately captured the imagination of the public and resonated with its comical images. The campaign has made the brand immensely popular even though the comic character does not particularly exhibit any association with Vodafone. Replace the callout of Vodafone with that of any other mobile operator, and the commercials would have the same meaning.

---

[27]Screenshot from "Vodafone zoo zoo ads all in one—All 25 Vodafone IPL ads," *zoozoofans.* May 19, 2009. https://www.youtube.com/watch?v=efRNKkmWdc0&feature= youtu.be, (accessed June 25, 2018).

It is a popular notion that during difficult times, people should back their strengths. That is exactly what one can observe the advertising industry doing. To tackle its existential crisis, it has to propagate itself, and to propagate itself, it is choosing to exploit the full potential of its advantages and strengths. The question that needs to be pertinently asked at this stage is why, in the first place, has this need for self-propagation arisen? Is it just about the existential paradox that we talked about, or is there something else to this story?

Attribute 6: Need for Self-Propagation

Indian commercials have evolved over the years along similar lines as has Indian society. Going back to the preliberalization era, when India was still under the protectionist regime, industries and products were not only inferior but fraught with inefficiencies. Then look to 1991, when our former finance minister, Manmohan Singh, directed reforms that changed how India looked at the world and, more importantly, how the world looked at India and Indians. We become geostrategic as global players when foreign direct investment (FDI) was introduced in many sectors and global competition began creeping in. Thus, Indian firms had to react aggressively to stay afloat in this stiff global competition. Learning from the dismal past, it became very important for India and the Indian society to put forward a good front, which required packaging their products and even themselves in a way that looked aspirational and competitive globally. With globalization came newer products and newer means of promotion, most noticeably multinational corporations and television sets, that opened up huge new platforms for industries to attract customers through television advertisement.

Advertisements in the 1990s in India very much reflected the Indian way of packaging and selling products and services to the world by appearing "aspirational." The focus was on *positive illusion enforcement* wherein the products' features were highlighted and most of them exaggerated to give them a greater packaged look. Take the case of the Nirma washing powder commercials in the 1990s with its famous jingle "*Dudh si safedi Nirma se aayi, Rangeen kapda bhi khil khil jaye*" (translation: *Milk like Cleanliness Comes with Nirma, Colorful Clothes Too Brighten Up*). Thus, an indigenous product was made "aspirational" by filling the commercial with features of making clothes as white as milk and how every Indian woman prefers Nirma, be its high foam content or whitening capability. Gradually, advertisements began to show women from different regions of the country using the product, as the intent was to showcase the detergent as the Indian washing powder.

In another commercial for the refined edible oil Dhara, a child leaves his home in anger and, even after repeated requests by his grandfather, does not show any willingness to come back home. It is only when the grandfather reminds him of *jalebi* (an Indian sweet) made in Dhara cooking oil that the child is convinced to come back and once again enjoys the *jalebi* with the whole family. Again, the focus of the commercial is on the features of the product and how it packages Dhara oil as a means to make great food.

Both the commercials over exaggerate features of the product they advertise, yet both products and their commercials received major acceptance, since the people and the society were accustomed to using the same technique to reposition themselves in front of the global business world.

Consider also the example of the famous *Hamara Bajaj* (translation: *Our Bajaj*) campaign. Each of its advertisements is full of symbols of progressiveness. Shots such as cruising through rough terrain, through industrial backgrounds, through ethnic settings—the progressive and technical yet Indian culture dominant visuals infiltrate the narrative backgrounds. These narratives were the Indians' ways of telling the world—we are coming and you better be ready for us. All along, it was all about packaging; India was all about packaging and selling itself; Indians were all about packaging and selling themselves to world.

Note: These presented narratives were developed by three different agencies: Nirma was by Purnima Advertising, Dhara by Mudra Communications, and Bajaj by Lowe Lintas.

However, times changed. During the 2010s, India left its "direct-aspirational" image far behind, and was now seen as the land of opportunity by the world. From a labor-centric region, India repositioned itself into a consumer-centric profile, where Indians were no longer aspiring to arrive, but now confident to make choices and also "position" options for the rest of the world to choose from. The old way of repackaging and over exaggerating themselves phased out, and people started looking at the substantiality of the product rather than the packaging itself. People started looking under the surface of the politicians' promises. The insecurity of the 1990s was replaced with confidence; the "appeal" India as a developing consumer was replaced with India as an emerging market that produces ideas, concepts and, above all, objects for global exchange.

A similar shift happened in the preferences for advertisements, too: from "appeal" to "ideas" to "substance." The exaggeration and superficial narratives of the commercials no longer appealed to the substance-seeking audience. Thus, there arose the need for the industry to find a way to redirect. As we have explained earlier, the communication measures were to delink the product from the advertisement. And by doing that, we arrive at our crucial phase in argumentation: how a nation changes course in advertisements as it transitions from a labor-centric market to that of a consumer-centric market.

Contemporary Positioning through Advertisements: The Disruptive Strategy Contributed by the Political Transitioning of Developing Sites to Emerging Markets

In the era of consumerism and in a market that has transitioned from a labor-centric global site to a consumer-centric global market, we would like to introduce a second paradox that plagues the advertising agencies today. This paradox is the **Irrelevant Relevance Paradox**. The very attempts by advertising agencies to stay relevant—by delinking the commercials from the products and services to appeal to the "intellectual masses"—is leading to their becoming irrelevant because people today are looking for substance, and ironically, commercials are merely cover-up narratives.

To add to the paradox, we point to the fact that advertisements have, in general, *flattened* brands as opposed to *differentiating* brands— something that they were meant to do. What do we mean by that? Simply put in today's times, advertising products or using the services of an advertising agency has ceased to provide any advantage to the brand. Commercials have been able to unintentionally provide level-playing field for everyone. A Reebok can position itself as a brand at par with an Adidas, by just advertising on the same platforms. As a consumer, if I see both Reebok and Adidas advertising themselves, I might tend to view them more equally than they actually are. **Thus, advertisements have become the non-discriminating medium or the lens through which every brand would seem to be on an equal footing. And more significantly, publicity image equalizes the first-world products with the emerging market products, too!**

> **RH7**: *The Irrelevant Relevance Paradox: Advertisements today are just a tool of parity, and not differentiation, both politically and commercially, for big and small brands and even for first and emerging worlds.*

The Road Ahead for Ad Agencies: Applied Lessons for Global Markets

In our view, the road ahead for advertising agencies and the industry would be shaped by two main forces—the growing irrelevance of advertising and the rise of the social media. We see this new phenomenon as a fight by advertising to stay the most preferred and desirable form of promotion in the Indian brands' minds, both locally and globally. What then is the future?

Applied Lesson 1: The Incumbents

Make yourselves a necessity like consulting firms

The key resource for any advertising agency is its people—the creative workforce that has the ability to shape the ideas of the society. However, how much of these skills are specific only to the advertising industry? Not much, we contend. That is also supported by the recent venture of Ogilvy & Mather into the filmmaking space. The recent documentary "Escape Fire: The Fight to Rescue American Healthcare," which premiered at the Sundance Film Festival, is just a start.[28] If there was any doubt about our contention on the irrelevance of such agencies, *Huffington Post* leaves

---

[28]https://www.imdb.com/title/tt2093109/news, (accessed August 10, 2018).

nothing to doubt. The article by the *Post* mentioning the release and the premiere was titled "Ad Agencies like Ogilvy Produce Documentary Films, Seeking Prestige and Payoff," which clearly hints at the need for such agencies to venture into new areas to seek prestige, given how irrelevant the advertisement domain has become.

Any futuristic direction for the *incumbents* is to leverage their ability to be the parity agents in the society of brands. The nature of work and client engagement of advertising agencies is too similar to the consulting industry to be ignored. Consultants are helping their clients with strategy, and advertisement agencies help with creative content. The most interesting and the most instrumental factor in such industries is the *absence of counterfactual arguments.* As a CEO hiring a consulting firm for my company, one can never know what could have been. How would the results have been if the company had not hired the consultants? Nobody can tell, and that is exactly what the consulting industry has been leveraging over the years. They have been successfully able to raise the stakes for their clientele—the risk of losing is high if you do not hire us, so you better do it. Moreover, since all other players are consulting them, just for the parity sake, each one ends up doing the same. The same analogy can be applied for advertisement world where firms may doubt but are not sure whether present commercials really are adding anything to their product sales, but they cannot risk going without them in danger of losing hard-earned customers. They therefore continue giving advertising agencies work just to remain in parity with other firms. There is a great lesson here on *how to convert yourself from a luxury to a necessity.* That, in a nutshell, captures what we are proposing for the advertising industry—make yourself a necessity and then leverage on that, leaving no question of irrelevance or obsolescence. Tie your relevance to the relevance of the brands.

Applied Lesson 2: New Entrants

Disrupt

A new entrant in the advertising industry faces the usual choice that any entrant would face in any industry—to follow or to disrupt. To follow would entail indulging in self-propagation, continuing with the delinking of advertisements and products, and at the same time diversifying into newer avenues of media or content creation. The more interesting and bold option would be to disrupt—change the rules of the game altogether. Such a disruption would require the creation of a completely new domain of advertising, using the latest trends to the company's advantage. Let us propose a few strategies here.

Disruptive Strategy I: Creation of a Repository

Delinking is rampant, advertisements are not being made specific to the product, and consumers a lot of times end up watching commercials that are not relevant to them. How can we tackle all three of these problems in one go? Let us think of a scenario where the delinking takes its extreme form—so much so that the products are actually being placed into the advertisements. In this scenario, the advertisement agencies can actually look to create repositories of advertisements, later to be used by brands to have focused advertising. Take for instance a company such as Procter & Gamble. It has innumerable brands in India, all of which is not relevant or is not targeting the same consumer. Here is where the repository comes in. An advertisement agency can create a commercial for P&G to place its product or brand into it according to the consumer in question. So there is one commercial—but when targeting one consumer group, P&G shows Product-A in that commercial and when targeting another group, it would show Product-B, both in the same commercial itself. Thus, the advertisement becomes the background or the mold into which products would be fitted.

Disruptive Strategy 2: Preempt Medium-Specific Narratives

Give Yourself Goosebumps, Choose your lure!

The advertising industry has always been disrupted by the specific availability of technology at various inflection points. Four major advances that made a huge impact on advertising are printing press, radio, television, and the Internet. It is interesting to observe how these transitions have taken place. Each phase had its specific set of advantages, and when the transition happens, it would take a while for the existing advantage to give space to newer spaces provided by the medium. In other words, *one medium feeds into another medium initially, with the former evolving itself over time eventually.*

For instance, during the early stages of radio, the advertisements were just print posters that were read aloud on the radio. Over time, the radio advertisements became more like speeches delinked from the printed texts. Similarly, during the early stages of television advertising, commercials were merely speeches supported by video in the foreground. Later, the advertisements took the form of stories and dialogues, leveraging on the capabilities of television. With the advent of the Internet, we believe the transition to the medium based advertising is yet to take hold. We are still sharing television ads on YouTube and Facebook, instead of medium-specific content. However, very soon history will repeat itself, and the Internet will be free of its dependence on television advertisements. There will be medium-specific, that is, Internet-specific content creation, leaving television behind, only to be overtaken by another medium in the times to follow. So, if we know this transition will happen sooner or later, what opportunities does it provide?

In the 1990s, Goosebumps was a large selling horror fantasy series. The author introduced a new series of books under the name "Give Yourself Goosebumps." These books had a footnote at the end of every page, wherein the reader could choose one among the options available and go to the corresponding page to continue the story. Similarly leveraging on the two-way communication of the Internet, we feel that advertisements in the future will be very user-input based. If a particular customer requires advertisements on product attribute, the corresponding commercial is shown, while if someone is interested in the story behind the product, then that commercial is shown. In this way, the advertisement agencies will be able to leverage the power of the Internet without compromising on their resources. To conclude, as McLuhan reminds us, *"Control over change would seem to consist in moving not with it but ahead of it. Anticipation gives the power to deflect and control force"* (McLuhan).[29]

---

[29]https://personalduediligence.com/2017/01/03/control-over-change-would-seem-to-consist-in-moving-not-with-it-but-ahead-of-it-anticipation-gives-the-power-to-deflect-and-control-force-marshall-mcluhan, (accessed August 10, 2018).

The question, however, remains—we have advertisements galore, *but for whom?* So the persuasive strategy for a disruptive global market now has to result from a "parity–medium" leveraging template of megaeconomic and geostrategic influencing intention, as summarized in Figure 5.12.

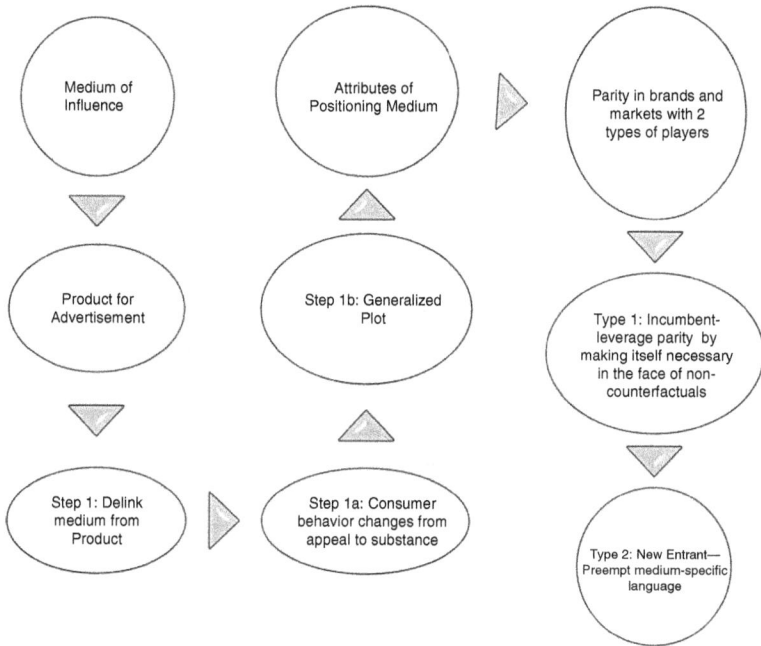

Figure 5.12 The "parity–medium" leverage template

Epilogue[30]

The authors brilliantly develop a new and contemporary advertising consultancy template—parity or medium leverage [P/M] template. The main premise is that current advertising practice is on a parity–medium interface. Parity, because advertisements are an effect, is necessary but irrelevant; all brands can replace each other through the advertisement medium, even among first-world and emerging market positions. At the same time advertisement language has to preempt the language of the new medium—that of the social media (Internet of Things).

---

[30]Contributed by Pragyan Rath, Communications, Indian Institute of Management Calcutta.

So, what happens to publicity in publicity images? The emerging market strategy in the era of the labor-centric global positioning had been the "genre" narrative of "aspirational sentimentality": the Indian ethos appeal in the hope of arriving as the future geostrategic global center of decision-making. Thus, the advertising agencies became repositories of cult value—the Indianness as a global ritual. Each consumer was part of the historical testimony of that cult value—of that time and space of a rising Indian aspiration—to be like and one of the top economies of the world. The consumer was in that optical space of experiencing the appeal of that "aspirational sentiment"–absorbed by the sentimental value of the social instrument of international progress, the social significance of being part of a rising world economy; an India that was trying to build its global aura, cruising far away from its local postindependence stance. The advertisement narratives of the time reflected these values, produced by magical hidden centers of cult productions—the architects of international differentiations on a global platform—the Indian differentiation on a multinational platform. The advertising agencies were seen as magicians. Thus, an era of hierarchical ritualism began, in which Ogilvy and Lintas, and a few others gained "cult" stature. Consider the parallel connections between consultants and ad agencies:

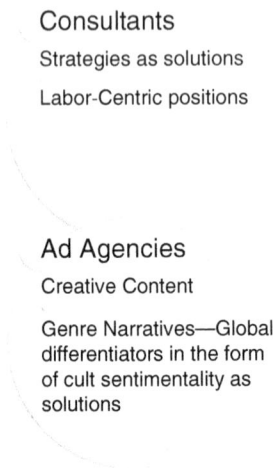

Consultants

Strategies as solutions

Labor-Centric positions

Ad Agencies

Creative Content

Genre Narratives—Global differentiators in the form of cult sentimentality as solutions

We call this relationship the cult era for advertising agencies in the publicity matrix for the labor-centric world economic position as shown in Table 5.3.

Table 5.3 *The cult era of Indian publicity images and its producers*

Creative content	Spectator consumer	Consumer affirmative logic			Producer	Economic value	Value for consumer-ism	Apperception
		Signifier	Signified	Pose				
Genre Narrative	Aspiring Indian middle class: contemplative	Objects converted into sentimental morality (India rising/shinning)	Indian community on a global platform	Sentiment	Ad Agencies as magicians and institutionalizers	Institutionalized capital	Cult Value	Optical—consumer as part of historical followership

As the center of labor transitions into a center of consumption, similar strategic and creative content also undergo transitions of positionings. Advertisements are "habits" now for a "distracted" audience; hence, any advertisement can replace any other, which on the one hand positions these narratives as redundant and on the other positions them as habitually relevant, as if any brand can have an advertisement—if Reebok can, so can I by the same agency. Thus, an agency is almost like a technology-producing entity—a surgeon who produces a platform of equal availability for anyone who wants to exhibit itself. As per the rules of an exhibition value, the narratives are no more about genres of sentimental value but additions of things to the Internet:

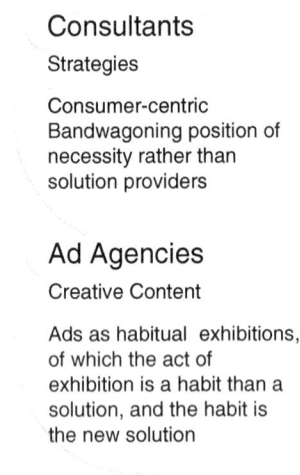

Consultants

Strategies

Consumer-centric
Bandwagoning position of
necessity rather than
solution providers

Ad Agencies

Creative Content

Ads as habitual exhibitions,
of which the act of
exhibition is a habit than a
solution, and the habit is
the new solution

We call this the exhibition era for advertising agencies in the publicity matrix for the consumer-centric world economic position as sketched in Table 5.4.

After all, McLuhan said, "medium is the message," but the authors here say, "medium is the leveler."

Table 5.4 The exhibition era of Indian publicity images and its producers

Creative content	Spectator consumer	Consumer affirmative logic			Producer	Economic value	Value for consumerism	Apperception
		Signifier	Signified	Pose				
Still Life Narrative	Diaspora	Common objects into ideations	Consumer in general	In a habitual position of exhibition	Ad agencies are surgeons and technicians	Objectified capital	Exhibition value	Tactical—consumer in direct and also immersive interaction

Bibliography

Benjamin W., and J. Underwood. 2008. *The Work of Art in the Age of Mechanical Reproduction*. London, UK: Penguin.

Berger, J., and M. Dibb. 1972. *Ways of Seeing*. London, UK: BBC Enterprises.

Bourdieu, P. 1986. *The Forms of Capital by Pierre Bourdieu*.

Derrida, J. 1967. *Writing and Difference*. Trans. Alan Bass. London, UK: Routledge.

Holt, D. 2004. *How Brands become Icons: The Principles of Cultural Branding*. Brighton, MA: Harvard Business Review.

Kornberger, M. 2010. *Brand Society: How Brands Transform Management and Lifestyle*. Cambridge, UK: Cambridge UP.

Marcuse, H. 1968. *Negations: Essays in Critical Theory*. NY: Free Association Books.

McLuhan, M. 1964. *Understanding Media: The Extensions of Man*. New York, NY: McGraw.

Ogilvy, D. 1983. *Ogilvy on Advertising*. New York, NY: Crown.

Rath, P. and A. Bharadwaj. 2018. *Communication Strategies for Corporate Leaders: Implications for the Global Market*. London, UK: Routledge.

Ryan, M.-L. 1991. *Possible Worlds, Artificial Intelligence, and Narrative Theory*. Bloomington, IN: Indiana UP.

About the Authors

Pragyan Rath is associate professor in communication in the Indian Institute of Management Calcutta (IIMC). She is developing the Narrative of Things in the lines of Internet of Things, thus innovating analytical models on market research. She has authored the following books: *The "I" and the "Eye": The Verbal and the Visual in Post-Renaissance Western Aesthetics* (Cambridge Scholars Publishing, 2011), *Communication Strategies for Corporate Leaders* (Routledge, 2018), and *Corporate Communication* (Cengage, 2018).

K. Shalini is a banker with State Bank of India (SBI) who has previously worked as a researcher in the Business Ethics and Communication Group at the Indian Institute of Management Calcutta (IIM-C) and has coauthored *Corporate Communication* (Cengage, 2018). A self-taught artist and a management graduate from National Institute of Technology, Durgapur (NIT), her research areas are in various business administration domains ranging from human resources to corporate communication.

Index

OTHER TITLES IN OUR CORPORATE COMMUNICATION COLLECTION

Debbie DuFrene, Stephen F. Austin State University, *Editor*

- *Managerial Communication and the Brain: Applying Neuroscience to Leadership Practices* by Dirk Remley
- *Communicating to Lead and Motivate* by William C. Sharbrough
- *64 Surefire Strategies for Being Understood When Communicating with Co-Workers* by Walter St. John
- *Business Research Reporting* by Dorinda Clippinger
- *English Business Jargon and Slang: How to Use It and What It Really Means* by Suzan St. Maur
- *Conducting Business Across Borders: Effective Communication in English with Non-Native Speakers* by Adrian Wallwork
- *Strategic Thinking and Writing* by Michael Edmondson
- *Business Report Guides: Research Reports and Business Plans* by Dorinda Clippinger
- *Business Report Guides: Routine and Nonroutine Reports and Policies, Procedures, and Instructions* by Dorinda Clippinger
- *Managerial Communication For Organizational Development* by Reginald L. Bell and Jeanette S. Martin
- *Managerial Communication for Organizational Development* by Reginald L. Bell and Jeanette S. Martin
- *Leadership Through A Screen: A Definitive Guide to Leading a Remote, Virtual Team* by Joseph Brady and Garry Prentice

Announcing the Business Expert Press Digital Library

Concise e-books business students need for classroom and research

This book can also be purchased in an e-book collection by your library as

- *a one-time purchase,*
- *that is owned forever,*
- *allows for simultaneous readers,*
- *has no restrictions on printing, and*
- *can be downloaded as PDFs from within the library community.*

Our digital library collections are a great solution to beat the rising cost of textbooks. E-books can be loaded into their course management systems or onto students' e-book readers. The **Business Expert Press** digital libraries are very affordable, with no obligation to buy in future years. For more information, please visit **www.businessexpertpress.com/librarians**. To set up a trial in the United States, please email **sales@businessexpertpress.com**.

www.ingramcontent.com/pod-product-compliance
Lightning Source LLC
Chambersburg PA
CBHW061310220326
41599CB00026B/4826

* 9 7 8 1 9 4 7 4 4 1 1 0 1 *